MARKETING & SALES ROI

What Is It Good For?

Pablo Turletti

 Copyright 2019 by **Pablo Turletti**
All rights reserved.

ISBN 13: 9781798230114
Library of Congress Control Number: 2017908623

Contents

PREFACE 7
ACKNOWLEDGMENTS 13
ABOUT ROI MARKETING INSTITUTE 16
ABOUT THE AUTHOR 20
INTRODUCTION 23
    WHAT CAN YOU EXPECT FROM THIS BOOK? 28
PART 1: ABOUT MARKETING & SALES PROJECT ECONOMICS 35
    CHAPTER I: WHY DO WE NEED TO CALCULATE THE ECONOMIC RETURN OF SALES ACTIVITIES & MARKETING PROJECTS? 36
        Sales & Marketing Accountability: A Critical Issue 36
        Why Is It Necessary to Calculate the Economic Return of Sales & Marketing Projects? 44
PART 2: HOW TO CALCULATE THE ECONOMIC RETURN OF SALES ACTIVITIES & MARKETING PROJECTS 51
    CHAPTER II: MEASUREMENT & EVALUATION IN MARKETING & SALES: THE ROI MARKETING MATRIX 52
        The Issue at Stake 52
        What Is ROI Marketing? 58
        ROI Marketing Guidelines 63
        Barriers to Implementing ROI Marketing 66
    CHAPTER III: THE ROI MARKETING MATRIX: THE THEORY BEHIND IT 74
        How Was It Created? 74
        Introduction to the ROI Marketing Matrix 76
        Levels of Evaluation & Measurement Dimensions 81
        The ROI Marketing Matrix Phases 84
        ROI Marketing Matrix Phase 1: The ROI Marketing Cascade 85
        ROI Marketing Matrix Phase 2: The ROI Marketing Ladder 146

PART 3: MARKETING & SALES ECONOMICS – WHAT IS IT GOOD FOR? 161

   CHAPTER IV: THE FOUR FUNCTIONALITIES OF AN ROI MARKETING MANAGEMENT MODEL 162

      Introduction *162*

   CHAPTER V: IS MY ORGANIZATION READY TO MANAGE SALES & MARKETING PROJECTS FOR PROFIT? 205

      Levels of Organization ROI Marketing Alignment *207*

   CHAPTER VI: ABOUT STAKEHOLDER MANAGEMENT – ANOTHER INTANGIBLE WORTH MEASURING 222

      What Defines a Stakeholder for Your Organization? *224*

      Who Are Your Stakeholders, Specifically? *225*

      What Is the Influence of Stakeholders on Your Organization? *229*

      What Is the Influence of Your Organization on Each Stakeholder? *232*

      How to Monitor Stakeholder Management Performance *236*

PART 4: USEFUL TOOLS 243

   ROI MARKETING MATRIX EXECUTION SCHEMA 246

   ROI MARKETING MATRIX OBJECTIVES TEMPLATE 248

   ROI MARKETING MATRIX 3WH DATA COLLECTION TEMPLATE 250

   ROI MARKETING MATRIX EVALUATION CHECKLIST 253

APPENDIX A: HOW TO GET STARTED 255

   HOW TO GET STARTED 256

TABLES & CHARTS INDEX 259

Case Studies

CASE I: ROI Marketing Cascade – About Alignment With the Pillars 88

CASE II: ROI Marketing Cascade – About Setting Objectives 97

CASE III: ROI Marketing Cascade – About Generating Relating Factors.. 114

CASE IV: ROI Marketing Cascade – About Monetary Conversion 137

CASE V: ROI Marketing Cascade – About ROI Sensitivity Analysis (Validation)... 142

Case VI: ROI Marketing Management – About ROI Sensitivity Analysis (Validation and Prediction – Predictive Modelling) 178

CASE VII: ROI Marketing Management – About ROI Analysis (Evaluation) 187

CASE VIII: ROI Marketing Management – About Business Intelligence (Planning) 195

CASE IX: ROI Marketing Management – About Using Marketing Economics for Sales Purposes 200

Preface

When I wrote my first book, *ROI Marketing: The New Performance Standard*, it was during 2007-2014, one of the longest periods of economic turmoil, and likely one of the most widespread without a war. Bubbles of all kinds burst around the world; companies struggled (and some still do) for economic sustainability, and many closed down completely. Unemployment erupted with its burning social magma, and new, alternative political parties and movements grew along with civic discomfort and unrest. This rough environment pushed companies of all kinds and in all territories to closely scrutinize the return on all projects and to become much more vigilant about their profitability in the short term. Marketing and sales initiatives were no exception to this quest for accountability.

Marketing is a very inexact discipline. It depends on perceptions that trigger behaviors based on a very broad set of parameters that range from emotional to rational and functional. There can be as many perceptions as consumers or clients behind them.

These and other intangibles seem to make gauging the economic results of marketing inaccurate, or, often, impossible. This apparent inaccuracy, and the fact that people outside of marketing feel qualified to discuss or question plans, make marketing a vulnerable and often unappreciated discipline within most organizations.

Today, marketing faces an even greater challenge, as technology enables – and even requires – new practices and knowledge. We've all heard the often-overused terms "big data" and "digital transformation." Millions of dollars and euros have been spent on a seemingly never-ending string of big projects that are supposed to generate new information and business intelligence that should help companies make wiser decisions. Many executives become frustrated after hiring big multinational consulting firms that have been working for years on new marketing data screens/dashboards/schemas that many don't understand, most don't want to use, and that seldom become operational at an organizational level. New reporting models, new jargon (which, in many cases, managers fear admitting they do not understand), and re-definitions of existing processes and procedures are only a few of the challenges that companies and organizations of all sorts face in this first quarter of the 21st century.

But what is all this change for? After all, technology is a tool, not a strategy. Digital transformation influences the way customers and consumers behave and the way organizations work. Big data refers to the actual capacity of retrieving humongous amounts of information at a very low cost, with high-speed processing capability, and extensive and very accurate querying potential. But big data and digital transformation are only tools to achieve certain goals – strategic goals. Most companies have limited the extent of their strategic goals to much shorter-term concerns that are driven by four main realities:

1. Consumers' erratic and ambiguous online and off-line behavior is making it almost impossible to define customer journeys.

2. The speed of change in several industries is increasing the pressure to innovate in processes that can generate a competitive advantage.

3. Newcomers, high-leverage game changers, are generating higher risks and uncertainties.

4. There is an increasing pressure for profitability.

These four realities are driving general management towards a short-term management mode. What matters is what we do now, which should somehow aim to satisfy one of the above-mentioned needs. Or at least, appears to possibly satisfy one of them...

So, how can technology (through digital transformation and big data) play a role not only in adapting to these new realities, but also in generating value in the longer term? Through the convergence between sales, marketing, and IT departments. Organizations need to understand that marketing and sales are the same: There are no sales efforts that do not belong to the marketing sphere, and there should be no marketing activity that does not have a clear, measurable impact on sales (short- or long-term). Even though marketing and sales activities seem to be undertaken in a separate fashion, they should have common goals, share indicators, work together, and use intertwined (if not the same) technical tools and systems.

This opens us to a figure who is emerging on many organization charts: the business data analyst. This is somebody who knows about business variables and management and can write or supervise data queries. Some of the most modern companies already understand this and have created a complete infrastructure that ensures this really happens. Some good examples include Airbnb, Google, and Amazon. In these companies, the business data analyst is the liaison between the IT world and the business world, in the same way ROI is the liaison between the marketing world and the business world. For managers and systems to be able to extract the business intelligence needed to make decisions that impact the short and long terms, they must speak with at least some common codes, goals, and indicators, or at a minimum, they must have someone who can act as a translator.

In order to become strategic to the business, marketing and sales efforts need to be visible in real economic terms. They must be visible in a robust, indisputable way.

In *ROI Marketing: The New Performance Standard,* I wrote that "calculating the return on any investment is straightforward. It is necessary to divide the net contribution (sometimes referred to as the *margin* or *net revenue*) by the investment and multiply it by 100 to get the percentage; the difficulty in marketing and sales lies in defining what the net contribution is and figuring out how to obtain the data that will determine it."

In recent years, many have spoken about the returns on marketing and sales investments, but very few were able to demonstrate how such returns were calculated (if it was done at all). Certainly, few, if any, contributed to the idea that these returns can be calculated in an accurate, robust, and credible way.

The ROI Marketing Matrix model showed the way to calculate the returns on marketing and sales investments with real case examples, finally demonstrating that it can be done. The methodology was actually used in different industries and on a broad set of project types (events, point-of-sale activations, trade, digital marketing, etc.). Knowing how to do it, however, is just the beginning of the process. Understanding how to use the results and conclusions is the final stage to getting the most out of it, making marketing strategic and relevant for the organization.

That is what this book is about: showing not only how to calculate the ROI of marketing and sales initiatives, but also the different approaches and functionalities that evaluating marketing projects and sales initiatives can bring, from the economic point of view, to businesses in general, and to professionals in particular.

Acknowledgments

Of course, none of the ideas, content, or experiences portrayed in this book would exist without the contribution of many people, companies, organizations, and experiences that I have come across during the last years in the market. ROI Marketing Institute (www.roimarketinginstitute.com) became the main source and international reference point for this topic. Through its interactions with several actors, in several countries and across many industries, it grew in its capabilities to learn and deliver, helping heavily in developing the contents of this book. Several project experiences, conferences, classes, webinars, cases, and papers produced at an international level also nourished these concepts.

There is a saying attributed to Walt Disney: "There are no good new ideas, only improvements of older ones." This book is no exception. After two decades of marketing and sales project experiences that gave birth to the ROI Marketing Matrix, a few more ideas were needed to chart the roadmap to optimizing the use of sales and marketing economics.

Many of these contributors are worth mentioning. It would be unfair not to mention all the clients and potential clients that dared to make visible the economic results of their marketing projects. I cannot mention their names for confidentiality issues, but they range from insurance firms and fast-moving consumer goods manufacturers to pharmaceutical companies, financial institutions, consulting firms, and even auto-racing and soccer teams. Thank you to each of them for being open to taking a new approach.

This work was also possible thanks to the people who worked on each and every one of those projects trying to understand and support a process that was not always that clear to them.

Thanks also to all the academic institutions that demonstrated interest in this topic, including IESE Business School, ESIC, IE Business School, Stockholm School of Economics, MIP Graduate School of Business in Milan, and the University of Jyväskylä in Finland. The academic world sharpens the robustness of the methodology and is a constant intellectual and factual challenge not only to the theory, but also to the way it is implemented in the real world.

Sometimes places can contribute to fresh ideas and inspiration. Long, crisp mornings facing the sea in Ribadesella (a small town in Asturias, in the north of Spain) cleared my mind and provided fresh air to feed new thoughts and reflections.

Most importantly, though, my main source of energy and devotion comes from the life-inspiring presence and thrust of my sons, and the much sought-after glory of feeling loved by my wife and being in love with her. Without them, nothing would have a sense, life would have no light, days would have no time, and ideas would have no meaning. To them I give my eternal love and devotion.

About ROI Marketing Institute

Responding to an always-increasing number of organizations searching for ways to make marketing accountable, ROI Marketing Institute (www.roimarketinginstitute.com) was founded to help companies and all sorts of institutions implement ROI Marketing within their structures, processes, and procedures. Its tools and services to achieve this goal are:

- Training and workshops: Through a customized set of courses, typically presented in one-day or two-day workshops, ROI Marketing Institute can prepare marketing and sales teams to adapt their processes and procedures to measure the financial return of their marketing and sales investments – their impact on the bottom line. The main objective of training is to transfer knowledge about the ROI Marketing methodology, how it works in real-world cases, and the theory behind it.

- Certification: ROI Marketing Institute is the only institution in the world that can award official ROI Marketing Professional and Corporate Certifications attesting to ROI Marketing Matrix competence, knowledge that has been demonstrated in the field and a proven capability to sustain it over time. Certifications add significant value to professionals' résumés (Professional Certification) and send a clear message to investors and shareholders about the cash flow management policy of a given business (Corporate Certification). Certification has two main objectives: to guarantee that professionals and organizations acquired the knowledge about the methodology and how it works, and to guarantee that they have demonstrated the capability and skills to put that knowledge into practice through real-world cases. With a Corporate Certification, companies of all sorts send a clear message to the market, stakeholders, and shareholders, showing that the organization embraces ROI Marketing as a management model for sales and marketing, and that ROI is the company's standard performance indicator. This shows that a company manages marketing and sales activities budgets with profitability in mind.

- Solution Implementation: For the most committed organizations, ROI Marketing Institute and its team of technicians can design, program, and implement in-house ROI Marketing solutions that will help the organization standardize the process of measuring the return of marketing and sales investments – making managing for profit a standard procedure. The main objective of this service is to ensure that managing marketing efforts for profits becomes part of the standard processes within the organization. We do so by using existing installed systems (ERP, CRM, etc.) as a source of data for a dashboard the allows the company to see the marketing and sales projects' efficiency and economic performance. The decision about whether or not to add a technological layer is based on the design of the organization's existing information infrastructure. ROI Marketing solutions can always be implemented without a technological layer, because many companies already have information systems that can manage the milestones and queries needed to evaluate projects from a profitability perspective.

- Consulting: ROI Marketing Institute operates with a network of international partners, offices, and analysts who carry out ROI studies for marketing and sales projects and campaigns for all types of organizations around the world. Consulting provides turnkey evaluation of projects and campaigns, delivering comprehensive reporting that includes, but is not limited to, diagnosis, evaluation, and recommendations. It helps organizations that either do not have available resources or do not have the skills to carry out ROI evaluations. Consulting gives clients the overall picture and first-hand experience with a real-world use of the power and deployment of the ROI Marketing Matrix model.

- <u>Auditing</u>: Many shareholders, CEOs, CFOs, general managers, managing directors, controllers, financial auditing firms, and anyone responsible for company profit and loss are always wondering what the actual economic contribution of marketing and certain sales initiatives is in many companies and organizations. For them, ROI Marketing Institute has developed an auditing service that delivers concrete numbers, as well as a comparative analysis portraying the company's marketing and sales project expenditures performance in relation to other business indicators, the industry, and competitors. The audit also delivers a set of recommendations for improvement and optimization. It uses internal and external indicators with a proactive, confidential, and objective approach to data. An audit can also set a baseline and follow up on reforms with an evolution report.

About the Author

Pablo Turletti is an internationally recognized expert on marketing and sales strategy, efficiency, and profitability. He shares how to set a higher standard for marketing accountability. He is the author of the books *ROI Marketing: The New Performance Standard* and *Marketing & Sales ROI: What Is It Good For?*, and he conducts keynote presentations, lectures, and workshops throughout the world.

Pablo developed the ROI Marketing Matrix model based on his more than 20 years of experience working with Fortune 500 companies and public organizations in the United States, Europe, and Latin America, helping them create marketing campaigns, improve marketing and management processes to increase efficiency, and achieve measurable bottom-line success.

Pablo is the founder and CEO of ROI Marketing Institute (ROIMI), which has offices in Miami, Lucerne, and Madrid. ROI Marketing Institute helps companies around the world improve the efficiency of their marketing investments by precisely measuring the economic return on marketing activities. It provides a broad array of services, including auditing, competency-building, implementation support, consulting, and research.

Pablo has served as a consultant for the European Union, as project director for the Italian government, as international vice president at three marketing agencies in the United States, as president of a leading marketing agency in Spain and Germany, and as a member of the boards of several companies in different sectors.

Several business schools – including The Stockholm School of Economics, the MIP Business School (Italy), the University of Jyväskylä (Finland), ESIC Business & Marketing School (Spain), and the Sustainability Management School (Switzerland) – have embraced the concept of ROI Marketing as part of their curriculum.

Introduction

This book is arranged in four parts for easy reading and understanding.

Part 1, "About Marketing and Sales Project Economics," offers an overall understanding of why we need to calculate the economic return of sales activities and marketing projects, what marketing and sales economics mean, why it is important, and how to use this concept to improve the overall organization and the sales and marketing departments. It also addresses the impact of these principles and practices on the professional career of marketing practitioners. In today's changing world, marketing and sales cannot be exempt or apart from the constant tornados that affect companies, countries, economies, management practices, and consumer behavior. The relationship between all of those entities is always changing; the pressure on management to adapt, plan, and react is increasing; and pressure for short-term results can lead to decision-making that doesn't take into account a company's long-term sustainability. This section will show you how to deal with the increasing need to financially evaluate marketing projects prior to investment, predict possible outcomes and scenarios, evaluate the actual economic results, and develop better and more efficient tools to optimize the use of financial resources when planning future marketing projects and activities.

Part 2 of this book, "How to Calculate the Economic Return of Sales Activities and Marketing Projects," offers a detailed explanation of how this revolutionary methodology was developed, the principles that rule its use, and the levers needed to obtain business intelligence and, ultimately, economic results from marketing and sales initiatives. In order to achieve robustness around sales initiatives and marketing accountability, it is necessary to use a systematic approach that can guarantee feasibility and credibility. The ROI Marketing Matrix model is used in more than 30 countries, in companies and organizations of all sorts, sizes, industries, sectors, and markets. This part of the book covers the guidelines, principles, and step-by-step approach to go from planning to execution, from setting objectives to evaluating results around sales and marketing projects and campaigns of all sorts. It covers the main concepts of ROI Marketing, including ROI Marketing Cascade, ROI Marketing Ladder, and the ROI Sensitivity Analysis that were initially developed in my first book, *ROI Marketing: The New Performance Standard*, and that have since evolved into a more efficient, more results-oriented, and easier-to-use methodology. Part 2 covers what we understand as economic return, the importance of a methodological approach to measuring it, the methodology itself, and a very useful tool to make an initial assessment about how close an organization is to being able to calculate the actual economic return on sales activities and marketing projects.

Part 3 of the book, called "Marketing and Sales Economics – What Is It Good for?," covers the four main functionalities that are required when measuring and planning for marketing and sales economics: validation, prediction, evaluation, and planning. Project or campaign validation aims to determine the threshold between making or losing money with the given marketing project. It predicts the economic scenario that will result from the project reaching its objectives, and it supports the go-no-go decision process. How many times do companies fail to see this threshold and launch promotions or campaigns that would lose money even if they sold 100% of the product on the shelves? How many times do marketers or sales directors actually calculate this economic threshold? The second functionality is prediction. The first step of this function is to find the break-even point of any marketing project. Salespeople and marketers should determine this threshold in terms of the project's commercial and market viability. The next step in prediction is to play with the controllable variables that can affect the economic outcome. By changing objectives, investment level, numeric distribution, timing, conversion ratios, etc., you can create scenarios for possible economic outcomes that support not only go-no-go decisions, but also defining and setting the initial conditions needed to achieve the desired results.

These initial two functionalities are pre-investment phases that produce one of the great positive consequences of managing marketing and sales activities with the business bottom line in mind: goal-setting and planning become results-oriented, rather than activity-based. The third functionality is the actual evaluation process. It entails, during and after execution, measuring the economic impact of marketing and sales projects and campaigns. Evaluation is based on the ROI Marketing Matrix. By deploying it, organizations are able to calculate the actual economic return of marketing and sales activities. Using stories based on real cases, this section of the book guides the reader in a step-by-step fashion from this evaluation all the way to the actual economic return of marketing and sales projects.

Last but not least, the fourth functionality, planning, is the one that probably generates the most value for the organization. Through evaluation cycles, companies will start gathering business intelligence that will help them plan future marketing projects and campaigns with a completely different perspective. Through historic conversion ratios (of marketing investment to profit), project return, and past experiences, salespeople and marketers will be able to start planning with the economics in mind, treating marketing and sales projects as an investment portfolio and reducing the likelihood of investing in projects that are not profitable for the company. The planning functionality requires an organization to acquire the ability to measure economic variables, raising the need to set rules and systems that will convert the economic evaluation of sales and marketing projects into standard procedures and reservoirs of information.

This third part of the book will show, with real-world cases from simple to complex, the challenges several projects started with and how they were solved.

Finally, Part 4, "Useful Tools," will share some useful tools and resources for those interested in becoming ROI Marketing practitioners.

Each part of the book is arranged in a reader-friendly format. Chapters are short and straight-to-the-point. Each chapter includes the questions it aims to answer, with reflecting points and conclusion/summary bullets that can be used as a quick reference for future consultation and easy implementation.

For confidentiality reasons, in most cases, whenever actual numbers are mentioned, the companies' names or sectors have been altered or changed, and whenever actual companies are mentioned, the real numbers have been altered.

What Can You Expect From This Book?

This book is a thorough guide for anyone involved in creating, producing, or implementing any type of sales and/or marketing project or campaign. Consumers have changed, and the world of business has been radically altered as well. The speed of change is continuously increasing, and expertise in any specific type of marketing, field, sales channel, distribution method, or media is a relatively diminishing value. By the time somebody becomes an "expert" in any medium, distribution network, or channel, this channel or medium has changed or new ones have appeared, forcing professionals to "relearn" and, in many cases, start from scratch. This book presents a results-based approach that begins with the end (profitable sales) in mind and collects data in several dimensions, from qualitative to quantitative, both from the communication/message point of view and from the business impact and return standpoint – regardless of the channel, sector, medium or activity at stake.

Through the knowledge acquired from this book, readers will be able to answer questions such as:

- What is the profit (not only revenue) generated by sales and marketing activities?
- What do consumers think about my company, brand, product, and/or service?
- What is the profitability of my distribution network?

- Is the way we manage our sales development and marketing budgets the most efficient one, from an economic point of view?
- What and how much do consumers know about my company, brand, and/or product?
- How do I report the economic results of my sales and marketing efforts, and which results should I report?
- What do I want stakeholders, clients and/or consumers to do with what they think and know about my company, brand, and/or product?
- What are the results of our call to action?
- What impact do clients/consumers have on my sales and costs?
- If I cannot measure the impact on sales or costs, how can I define the value as an intangible?
- How do I set the pricing of sponsorship opportunities?
- What are the economic benefits of sponsorships?
- How might a change in our distribution network affect our business results?

In this book, you will learn how to set objectives in six different evaluation dimensions (from communication to business-related matters, including return on investment); define key performance indicators (KPIs) that can unequivocally show the cause-effect relationship between what happens in the communications and marketing world and its impact on the company's bottom line; and collect and analyze the data to measure the real economic impact of your sales and marketing projects.

This book proposes a methodology that should allow sales staff and marketers to predict and measure the return (profit) generated by an individual project or a group of projects as a campaign. This methodology will work regardless of the type of project they are handling, including salesforce activation, events, social media, direct marketing, grassroots, digital marketing, sales and distribution action, point-of-sale activities, etc. This approach changes the focus from activity-based to results-oriented, from communication-based to communication- and business-impact-based, and from input-based (Gross Rating Points, opportunity to see, click-through ratio, cost-per-click, etc.) to output-based (ROI).

The focus then shifts away from measuring how many Gross Rating Points (GRP) you bought, the number of direct responses you received, unique visitors to a website, customer satisfaction, "likes" on Facebook, click-through ratio (CTR), opportunity to see (OTS), audience, and other activity-based and input-related measures. Instead, the focus shifts to measuring ROI. This is a unique type of comparable, usable, cross-functional data; it is a number representing money (not value) that will be in the pockets of the business and that the business can use, for instance, at the end of the month to pay its payroll. This book will describe when to use it and for what purpose.

There is no magic formula to calculate the economic return of sales and marketing projects, no black-box spreadsheet to plug data into. There is no one-size-fits-all matrix that will spit out the magic number. Nevertheless, you should not be deceived into discouragement by the complexity of the first time you try this method. There is a difference between complexity and difficulty. The first time you put an ROI evaluation into practice, it may seem complex, cumbersome, and maybe even impossible. The first time, you will need to shift paradigms and think in a different way. This always poses challenges (professional, personal, and organizational). The complexity derives from the lack of practice, precedents, adoption of new points of view, and unusual demands for information. But all this is far from difficult. Furthermore, after the first time an evaluation cycle is completed, practitioners will have set the first milestone of a new, more evolved, more strategic way of managing sales and marketing budgets. Once the first plans are in place for relating factors, monetization criteria, and data collection, it will be much easier and faster to conduct a second ROI evaluation. Both the need for an evaluation and the results of the evaluation will be more accepted at all organization levels.

In this book, I aim to present a method focused on building a credible process that generates value in financial terms, and that is simple, robust, feasible, accurate, and reliable. It approaches credibility directly through:

1. defined and clearly identifiable sets of data,
2. a systematic process approach, and
3. a set of standards and milestones.

This book also includes nine business cases to show how marketing economics is used to enhance business outcomes. Whenever necessary, clients' names and information have been disguised for confidentiality purposes.

The reader will see, in different scenarios, for different industries, and for a diverse mix of projects, the logic behind planning marketing activities for economic results.

The book explores the challenges of collecting data in a measurable way and linking it to profits. This will be an indispensable guide for marketers and salespeople who seek to understand more about the bottom-line accountability of sales and marketing-related projects and campaigns.

Summary bullets:

- From now on, you will always work in a changing environment. Become an expert in adapting!
- New questions require new answers.
- New answers require new ways of thinking and doing.
- Plan in a results-oriented fashion, rather than in an activity-based mindset.
- There is no magic formula to calculate the ROI of marketing.
- You will need to adapt the ROI Marketing model to your reality and environment.
- It may seem complex the first time, but it is never difficult!

Part 1: About Marketing & Sales Project Economics

Chapter I:
Why Do We Need to Calculate the Economic Return of Sales Activities & Marketing Projects?

Sales & Marketing Accountability: A Critical Issue

Depending on your generation, you may remember the movie *Jerry Maguire* (1996), in which Tom Cruise, playing a sports agent, was forced to scream, loudly, ridiculously "Show me the money!" on the phone to his last client after being fired from his firm. His only remaining client was pressing his desperate agent to remember, by screaming over and over, the most important and final outcome of his job: generating money. This is the scream that most general managers and C-level executives hear over and over, year after year, at board and shareholder meetings. This scream is translated also, and during the last 10 years more loudly, to VPs of sales and marketing, and marketing and sales directors around the world.

By now, we all know that profitability is not the only relevant thing to keep businesses alive. Positive returns, in the short term, do not guarantee by themselves the sustainability of a business. Many other factors play a role, from environmental and social sustainability to brand awareness, company reputation, investment policies, market conditions, distribution, and a long list of, etc. Yet, without sustained short-term profitability, the rest would not exist.

Without visibility of their real economic impact, marketing and sales efforts are perceived as an expense. The worldwide economic crisis that started in 2007 exacerbated the need to prove the actual monetary contribution of marketing and sales initiatives to the company profit and loss. The need to become more efficient and cut costs made marketing and sales expenditures permanently more volatile, as their value was re-examined and questioned. Marketing and sales plans started to be constantly revised, and budgets began to be treated as an adjustment variable at the organizational level.

But sales initiatives and marketing are as much a relevant and indispensable component of every business as finance, the supply chain, and human resources. Companies often measure the financial return of their positive cash flows, the benefits of their supply chain, and the productivity of their labor force. Very seldom do organizations determine, in monetary terms, the accountability of their marketing and sales efforts. In a broad sense, some of them do it, but in most cases, they certainly fail to evaluate the opportunity cost of their different projects and campaigns, as well as the real return (not just the sales variation) of marketing and sales investments.

This book aims to demonstrate that the contributions of most (if not all) sales and marketing projects and campaigns can be measured in real economic terms, and that these activities are an investment and, as such, we should be able to determine their economic return. For most sales initiatives and marketing investments, there is a way to calculate their return in profits.

Marketing has always been, and it will forever be, a discipline of communication. Companies communicate about their brand identity, their messages, their offers of products and services, their commitments to social and environmental sustainability, their information to investors, and for many other reasons. In all cases, this communication aims to prompt an immediate or later action by the receiver (client, consumer, stakeholder, etc.).

The key performance indicators (KPIs) for marketing and sales initiatives have traditionally been linked to this communications world in terms of their project/campaign inputs. These input-based indicators include measures such as impressions, visits, readers, attendance, responses, registration, adherence, recall, awareness, intentions, and so on. Marketing and sales initiatives are rarely evaluated in terms of their real economic returns. While in finance, the link to the business shows up in the profit and loss (P&L) account; in human resources, it is evident in productivity indexes. Where is the link to the business for marketing? There is no need to prove that sales activities and marketing are, if executed correctly and with efficacy, positive for organizations (long- and short-term), but without clear economic measurements, marketers and salespeople will always be measuring performance in terms of interactions and communication impacts. Without monetary values and results, companies will never be able to show whether they could have achieved the same sales and profits with less marketing or sales investment. They will also be unable to show the potential extra contribution of marginal investments in marketing or sales. The recently coined term "performance marketing," while results-driven, fails to show the contribution of marketing to the business in a quantitative economic fashion. Without an economic performance indicator, we will be honoring John Wanamaker's famous epitaph to marketing as a discipline: "Half the money I spend on advertising is wasted; the trouble is I don't know which half."

Managing marketing and sales project economics will help companies and organizations link marketing to the business in an accountable way. By using marketing economics, while keeping the essence of marketing in communication, companies will be connecting marketing to the bottom line reliably, accountably, and with plenty of resources to plan for future investments. Marketing budgets will be considered as investments rather than as adjustable variables or simply costs.

Regardless of the industry you are in, or the marketing discipline you work on, marketing economics offers a unique, cross-sector, cross-functional, and reliable way to show the contribution of marketing to corporate communication and to business in an accountable fashion: profits.

The same happens with sales initiatives. Arguably, they could be considered marketing activities, but for several reasons, companies keep making efforts to split marketing from sales, as if they were two different disciplines (when in reality, they have the same aims and scope).

So, why is it that most businesses are still not using sales and marketing economics as a standard? The reason lies perhaps in the fact that, while areas of the business like human resources, production, or finance have more accurate and credible measurable variables (interest, productivity, inventory, etc.) that can be directly related to economic outcomes, marketing and sales activities generally struggle to achieve this direct cause-effect connection.

Consider the most broadly used marketing medium: TV advertising. Literally billions of euros and dollars are spent worldwide advertising on TV every year. The standard measurable performance indicator is GRP (Gross Rating Point). As marketers know, GRP measures the size of the target audience supposedly reached through the ad. But in most cases, marketers fail to obtain, and general management does not demand, a direct connection between the impact of such investments and the business (generally sales or, better, profits). It is assumed, considering the classical theory, that, keeping all other elements of the marketing mix stable, the variation in sales can be attributed to advertising. In some cases, that may hold true. However, during the last 20 years, marketing and marketers have undergone a deep transformation, which includes the appearance of new media and channels. A complete revolution in consumer behavior began and is still occurring, together with an incredible increase in the speed of change of all kinds. The relative weight of advertising started to diminish – a trend confirmed by more than 20 years of decreasing relative investments in conventional media advertising. Other means of communication have come into favor, such as grassroots efforts, events, digital marketing, and social media campaigns, just to name a few. So too has the relevance of the only generally accepted standard of measurement, the GRP. After all, GRPs are something you buy, rather than something you get out of your marketing campaigns – so if you are a general manager or CEO, you shouldn't accept GRPs as a "result" of any campaign.

During the last decade, sales personnel and marketers have more incisively faced the challenge of demonstrating the value of their initiatives for the business, yet they struggle to show that value in monetary terms. Many ways of measuring return appeared or were proposed: intention to purchase, return on emotions, satisfaction, return on influence, reputation, return on impacts, etc. All of them fail to show marketing and sales activities' real economics.

This book proposes an answer to, and ways to deal with, the relevant and broadly presented question of what impact sales and marketing has on a company's profits. If sales and marketing need to be linked by their economic or financial nature and to show their economic contribution, the ROI Marketing Matrix this book will explain opens up the possibility of doing so. When used properly by marketing and salespeople, the Matrix can generate a new marketing and sales projects KPI standard: return.

Summary bullets:

- Show them the money!

- Business concerns are not only about economic sustainability, but also about social and environmental sustainability.

- There cannot be social and environmental sustainability without economic sustainability.

- Marketing and sales initiatives should be treated as investments, not as costs.

- Measure marketing by using economic indicators in addition to the usual interaction KPIs.

- Sales and marketing should be the same department.

Why Is It Necessary to Calculate the Economic Return of Sales & Marketing Projects?

With the reality of economic struggles, cost-cutting policies, and the need for short-term returns, accountability and efficiency must be addressed early and often in all new sales or marketing projects and campaigns. This book shows sales and marketing professionals and managers how to measure the success of their projects, campaigns, and communications initiatives (internal or external) with a common standard, cross-functional, cross-media, cross-channel profile of success, including the economic return that they generate.

Collectively, the output (rather than the input) measures gathered through the ROI Marketing Matrix model presented in this book will help organizations capture success patterns. These patterns represent qualitative and quantitative data taken from different levels and dimensions, reflecting both economic and non-economic outcomes.

Companies, public and non-for-profit organizations, associations, and managers of all types cannot afford to kick off marketing or sales projects without a perspective for a feasible profitability scenario and a clear evaluation plan. Shareholders and stakeholders do not accept subjective performance evaluations anymore; analysts and banks need better indicators for those activities that represent expenditures yet somehow have no visible impact on balance sheets. That is why there is a need to add more rigor and discipline to the way sales and marketing projects are launched and evaluated. The question at stake is not whether sales projects and marketing are good or bad – we all know both are good for the health and sustainability of the business, and necessary. The real underlying question is how to use budgets (a scarce resource) in the most efficient way, contributing to the maximum positive economic results, as well as how to define unbiased criteria to decide between various sales and marketing investments.

There is a growing need to know, prior to investment, whether a project will or will not make money if it achieves its goals. It is also necessary to understand just how much a sales or marketing project must influence sales to pay for itself. Businesses must also be able to predict possible outcomes and scenarios by changing the variables under control, as well as measure the actual economic impact in monetary terms in a robust and credible way. Finally, it is imperative to gather and use business intelligence to draw conclusions, judge performance, and plan future actions and projects with better chances of succeeding.

With its conservative standards and systematic approach, the ROI Marketing Matrix is CFO-friendly, board-friendly, and CEO-friendly. The results and conclusions obtained will facilitate the sales division and marketers in securing funding; building support for projects and campaigns; improving processes and procedures, as well as their relationship with general management, C-level executives, shareholders, and stakeholders. An important advantage of this process is that it is dynamic and focuses on improvement, while still aiming for economic results. If a particular project or campaign is not adding value, steps can be taken to make it successful. If an existing campaign is not working or it is considered "not successful," this process will reveal a clear diagnosis for why, which will help to improve it or provide justification for discontinuing it.

This book describes a credible, reliable process that can be used by organizations worldwide to plan for, and measure the success of, sales and marketing projects and programs in a variety of industries and markets.

At first quick glance, you may wonder: Is this just another book with another way to measure economic results that will create a lot of work for me, based mainly on assumptions? As you go through the pages, it will quickly become clear that it is not. This book will transform the way professionals and organizations approach and plan sales projects and marketing activities. It presents a management model that can become operational. You will soon see that the way we define "results" is not the same way many other books do. Numeric distribution, attendance, intention to purchase, satisfaction, listing, and visitors are not the results (output) generated by sales activities and marketing. They are its input. The broadly used communication-only and distribution, marketing, and sales model has died. Sales and marketing initiatives, as much as logistics, finance, and human resources, are business variables, and as such, general management and managers overall should not fail to show its contribution to the business in an accountable economic way, such as through cash flow and generated profit.

The ROI Marketing management model represents a way of putting marketing and sales activities under the business umbrella. It is not about what you do, how you do it, or where you do it; it is about how what you do impacts communications *and* the business, showing its value in cash while contributing also to social and environmental sustainability.

That is why now, more than ever, sales and marketing projects should be put under the microscope prior to, during, and after investing in and implementing them.

Prior to investment, sales and marketing professionals need to validate any project in terms of the following question: What will be the economic, social, and environmental impacts of my project if it achieves its objectives? Regardless of the answer to this first crucial question, managers should generate predictive models that shall allow them to also answer these questions: What is the break-even point of my project in terms of sales? Is it achievable? How would it affect results if I change some of the variables under my control?

Once the investment is made and the implementation of the project starts, sales personnel and marketers should be able to accurately and credibly measure its actual economic outcome. They should also be able to evaluate the very same project from different perspectives and variables, both tangible and intangible.

Finally, evaluation cycles will generate business intelligence that should be used for planning future projects in a much more accurate and efficient way, optimizing resources and managing for profits, with social and environmental issues in mind.

Summary bullets:

- Managers should know, prior to investment, whether their projects will make money or not if goals are achieved.

- Managers should know how much a project must influence sales in order to pay for itself and verify its commercial viability.

- For all sales and marketing projects, managers should attempt to measure their contribution to the business in economic terms. If it is not real money, it is not ROI.

- Sales and marketing professionals should build predictive models to generate possible scenarios changing variables under control.

- ROI is the new standard performance indicator for marketing and sales activities.

- Measurement processes and procedures should be simple, robust, feasible, accurate, and reliable.

- Evaluation cycles will generate business intelligence that will not only monitor the contribution of a past project, but will also help to optimize resources when planning future ones.

Part 2: Calculating the Economic Return of Sales & Marketing Projects

Chapter II:
Measurement & Evaluation in Marketing & Sales: The ROI Marketing Matrix

The Issue at Stake

Measuring and evaluating results in sales and marketing projects and campaigns has been and still is a hot topic at conferences, in webinars, articles, and business schools. It is also one of the most controversial and open-to-discussion issues among managers of all sorts and in all industries. It is hard to find common ground and criteria that can help to judge positioning, acquired knowledge, and interactions comparatively among different projects, which have different media, different channels, a broad set of communication objectives, several KPIs, and an elusive link to business impact. Professionals and organizations struggle to find, use, and gain consensus about ways to reliably measure and evaluate sales and marketing projects. Furthermore, it is commonly accepted, even by general management, that it is difficult to measure or evaluate marketing projects and campaigns from a business-impact point of view. Thus, there is rarely an answer to the question "How much money did this campaign generate?" Even worse, the question is often never posed because most assume that it is not possible to measure it reliably.

Although interest in the topic has been heightened and much progress has been made (thanks in great part to access to new technologies and the advent of digital marketing), it is still an issue that challenges most sales and marketing departments, pressuring many managers. Regardless of the position taken on the issue, the calls for measuring and evaluating the real economic returns of marketing and sales activities are intensifying.

The dilemma surrounding the economic evaluation of sales activities and marketing is a source of frustration for many senior executives. Most professionals realize that marketing investments and sales initiatives are needed, but struggle to find evidence of their actual accountable economic impact on the business. Marketing, then, becomes an expense, one that is very easy to adjust, and is rarely considered an investment. The return expected from marketing and sales activities is often connected to variables linked to the four pillars of marketing (product, price, placement, and communication), and although a certain degree of business impact can be inferred, in many cases, it is not quantified and mostly never accounted for. Until now, it's been a daunting, rarely achieved task to move up on the scale of value to really show the money that marketing generates for the business.

The trend in evaluating marketing and sales activities has been to measure certain project inputs that, while showing value, fail to reveal an impact on the business's cash flows. This has lately been called "performance marketing." But, while these inputs are part of the consequences of marketing and sales activities and are certainly a relevant set of data, they fail to show any direct influence on the business from the financial point of view. Evaluations of sales and marketing activities need to show this influence. After all, sales and marketing use the financial resources of the company, so why shouldn't they be measured against these resources? Marketers and salespeople frequently face some of the following questions:

- How can I link the results obtained from communications and sales interactions to cash generated for the business?
- How can my measurement and evaluation gain credibility in the eyes of stakeholders?
- What if results are negative? What is the impact on my career? Is there any risk for me?

Unable to find clear and concrete responses to these questions, the industry shifted toward less-demanding ways of evaluating marketing and sales activities. Those standards became accepted but are far from meeting the expectations and information needs of C-level executives and business managers. It is necessary to move from measuring only reach and impact and to take a deeper dive into key business variables, especially profit.

This book demonstrates how to measure the contribution of marketing in an economically accountable way. ROI is about money; it is the expected surplus of money generated after conducting a business practice. Measuring economic ROI is the only way to show that marketing and sales activities are an investment rather than an expense. Based on this need for accountability, during the last several years we've seen a growing trend of evaluation procedures that move toward:

- Measuring qualitative variables (online reputation, "likeability," positioning, etc.)
- Using digital tools, media, and channels to measure marketing impact (social media, mobile devices, apps, etc.)
- The use of new marketing tools and technology (geolocation, new POS technologies, near-field communication, RFID, etc.)
- New measurement standards (click-through-ratio, "likes," unique visitors, cost per click, etc.) replacing or broadening the traditional standards of GRP (Gross Rating Points) and OTS (opportunity to see)
- Consumer involvement and influence through "gained media," "social mention," "online reputation," etc.

None of the above are outputs. All are inputs generated by the organizations' communications efforts, the influence that marketing and sales activities have on the way people think about companies' products and services, what they know about them, and what they do as part of the call to action (register, "like," visit the website, download the application, talk about the company or product on social media, etc.). Few of these (if any) really show, by themselves, an impact on business variables, such as cash flow or profit. Furthermore, none of the above can show, in a reliable and generally accepted way, how much money a project generated for the business.

Thankfully, by having this book in your hands, you are about to change that.

The use of ROI is emerging as an essential part of many measurement and evaluation systems. It is a fast-growing metric on most organizations' wish lists. But only a few organizations really measure ROI in sales and marketing projects, and almost none of them have adopted an ROI Marketing management model.

Summary bullets:

- Don't be deceived: The actual economic return of sales and marketing projects and campaigns can be calculated.

- Performance marketing is not equal to ROI Marketing.

- Do not settle for less-demanding marketing metrics – insist on business-related metrics.

- No money, no ROI. Value does not equal return.

- Adopt the real economic return (ROI) as a standard.

What Is ROI Marketing?

ROI – return on investment – defines the value generated (return) by a given expenditure (the investment) after discounting for the expenditure. Its definition helps to guide future investment decisions, because it can determine future cash flows and opportunity costs of investments. This works for all sorts of investments. However, financial staff members generally work out ROI calculations for infrequent capital goods expenditures, with a long-term impact, usually of large sums of money. Net present value (discounted future cash flows) is also usually included in the calculations.

Marketing investments have a much different decision-making process and pattern, as do sales campaigns. They generally have a shorter-term horizon and cycle (usually one year or less), in many cases involving smaller amounts of money, and therefore, they occur with a much higher frequency. Yet, marketing is money spent with the expectation of generating a positive return. And, in aggregate, an organization's marketing investment tends to be much larger than its capital goods investment. In addition, marketing projects and/or sales campaigns are scalable and have many different possible variations. This adds a new dimension to the concept of marginal investment and makes ROI evaluation and projection a much more relevant and impactful indicator. Marketers can do a $1 million advertising campaign or use the same creativity to do a $5 million campaign. They can use this amount of money to aim for the same goals through a completely different set of media or channels. They can decide to invest this money in grassroots promotions, for instance, or a combination of print advertising campaigns. Furthermore, marketers can use the same type of media or channels to generate different outcomes. Financial and production personnel cannot use two completely different machines to produce the same product or decide to use the same machine to produce three different products with the same ease that marketers can change either goals or means. This makes marketing and sales investment decisions a much more complex process. Marketers, salespeople, and the marketing discipline need a better way of gauging their projects' economic impact, in order to increase credibility and raise the strategic value of marketing within an organization.

This is what ROI Marketing is about. It is a sales and marketing management model that implies changing the way marketers:

- Plan marketing
- Execute marketing
- Evaluate marketing
- Analyze impact
- Report marketing results

It does not mean revolutionizing the way we do marketing, but rather, evolving towards a more relevant, accountable, and impactful (for the economics of the business) sales and marketing management model. It represents a way of managing marketing and sales budgets.

Deploying the ROI Marketing management model leads to:

- A more relevant-to-the-business marketing strategy
- Happy top executives with better decision-making capabilities
- Improved bottom-line capabilities
- A better position for negotiating marketing and sales budgets
- Connecting and aligning the marketing department with the business development/sales department
- Better professional sales and marketing skills
- Continuous improvement in sales and marketing practices

A simplified sales or marketing campaign cycle would usually show a path like this:

Objective-setting => project planning => project deployment => consumers' or clients' behavior => effect measurement => conclusions and assumptions => new-project planning

The ROI Marketing model adds a new dimension, contributing to the way marketers and sales personnel carry on the planning, execution, evaluation, and analysis of sales and marketing projects. It does not change the campaign cycle; it changes the way the cycle evolves and the results it obtains. Practicing ROI Marketing means that marketing departments will move from planning based on past and future budget allocations to planning based on past and future returns (measured and expected).

What difference does it make whether we practice ROI Marketing or not?

Table 1: Marketing & Sales Without ROI vs. Marketing & Sales With ROI

Marketing & Sales Activities Without ROI	Marketing & Sales Activities With ROI
Activity-based	Results-oriented
Several KPIs for different projects	One KPI for all projects
Proven impact on communication only	Proven impact on communication and business
Marketing & sales initiatives = costs	Marketing & sales initiatives = investments

Summary bullets:

- ROI Marketing is a management model, not a system.

- ROI Marketing is not a post-execution analysis – it is planning to evaluate and manage for profits.

- ROI Marketing serves both to evaluate and to generate business intelligence.

- In order to implement ROI Marketing, sales and marketing departments must work in a convergent fashion.

ROI Marketing Guidelines

As I've previously said, no money means no ROI. Does this mean that by using the ROI Marketing Matrix companies will be able to measure the ROI of *all* projects and campaigns? Certainly not. There may be projects whose aim is not to garner clear, accountable profits in the short term. Take, for instance, corporate donations. We can establish a connection between how a company's charitable giving influences purchase decisions in a relevant, statistical way in order to infer the impact of a donation on sales for a given period. But the corporate team that originated the idea of donating may have done so not just to make a profit, but also – or more importantly – to give society a clear message about the corporation's commitment to social or environmental sustainability. Through the donation, the company is talking to society about its values and principles. This, in the end, may influence purchasing decisions, but the aim of the donation is not such. The questions then are: Is it worth it to measure the ROI of this donation? Was obtaining a positive financial return one of its goals?

There might be other cases where evaluating a project from the ROI Marketing perspective would simply be too costly (remember that the cost of measuring ROI is part of the marketing or sales investment), making the evaluation impractical. However, in some cases, it will still make sense to run an ROI Sensitivity Analysis, which uses predictive modelling to anticipate possible outcomes (see Chapter III, page 141) and offers a pre-investment check on the potential of a given project to deliver positive or negative returns.

One thing is certain: In either of the above-mentioned cases, there may not be an ROI figure at the end of the project. This does not mean that it's impossible to measure its impact on the other ROI Marketing dimensions, such as impact of messages, interactions, and costs. There should not be any blind investment in the hopes of some sort of intangible impact. Even if only "soft data" can be collected, impact can still be measured. It is not a financial impact, not an ROI, but it is still an impact. In many cases, this may be the aim of a project.

For all other projects aiming to have a positive impact on the bottom line of the business, the following *seven guidelines* will provide integrity to the overall process of evaluating and measuring marketing and sales projects.

ROI Marketing Guidelines:

1. Marketing and sales efforts and plans should be *aligned* with the business mission, vision, and global objectives – in other words, the business pillars.
2. It is not possible to measure the ROI of any project without previously setting the *right objectives*.

3. *Plan* to collect, analyze, and extract conclusions from data.
4. Analysts should use *significant data* (truly and consistently representing the outcome it relates to).
5. All data used should follow the most *conservative criteria*. Use the worst-case scenario.
6. To reach an ROI figure, it is necessary to use *financial* connections and measures (no money, no ROI).
7. *Validate* methodology with the reporting level prior to showing results. Build credibility and acceptance prior to reporting results.

In all cases, keep in mind that there is a certain possibility of measuring the ROI in any marketing project. It is just a matter of time and resources.

Barriers to Implementing ROI Marketing

Measuring the actual ROI of sales activities and marketing projects can be difficult and complex the first time you undertake it. With rigor and relevance, however, a good system of practices can be put in place in such a way that sales and marketing do not suffer a revolution, but rather, an evolution towards becoming more accountable and more impactful divisions within the organization. What are the main barriers that ROI Marketing faces in most organizations?

- *A clear definition of ROI*

How many times have we heard about ROI when talking about marketing? Certainly many. But how many times have we heard the same definition for such a simple acronym? I am sure you may have heard about performance marketing, ROI on emotions, return on credibility, and a long list of "returns" that somehow show the value (in most cases, never monetary) generated by a marketing activity or project. But this variety of interpretations and lack of a clear definition unwittingly hinder the credibility of the concept of marketing ROI and of marketing overall. In the case of sales activities, although it may seem simpler, managers usually fail to define an actual return of such activities and content themselves with measuring numbers that don't actually affect the business. Take the insurance industry, for instance. Here, the key performance indicator is often "policy underwriting," which means that an insurance contract has been issued. But this doesn't mean that the policy was paid for, nor does it mean that the company profited from it.

- *The idea that measuring real ROI is too complex*

Evaluation can be difficult because projects are different, they use different media and channels, and industries and consumer segments vary vastly. Implementing an ROI evaluation process across multiple projects and/or campaigns may sometimes be quite complex. The challenge is to develop models that are theoretically sound, yet simple, credible, and usable. The overall idea is to build the measuring architecture starting from project/campaign planning in such a way that, during implementation, the methodology adapts to the project and not vice versa. In the end, ROI Marketing is a way of thinking about and doing marketing. The first time you use ROI marketing, with no or limited processes in place and a lack of references, setting up the measuring criteria and gaining internal momentum may be cumbersome. But soon, the efforts will pay off, and after the first cycle of evaluation, it will turn into a much smoother and indisputably valuable procedure.

- *Lack of rigor and relevance*

As previously stated, ROI is a popular topic for many conferences, articles, events, and business schools. Lots of people are talking about it in various ways and using broad and light definitions. I once read that in marketing, ROI equals ROA (return on assets) or that ROI in the events world is measured in emotions or experiences. Can you imagine your end-of-the-month payroll paid with *emotions*? Worse yet, many methodologies or systems in place lack the systematic, conservative approach needed to make them robust and credible.

- *Lack of standardization*

The very same nature of sales and marketing activities makes it possible to measure the same thing in a variety of ways (attribution models), or to measure different things the same way (measuring impressions, for instance). Without corporate common standards, each project or campaign director, each brand or product manager, or each division within the marketing department (trade marketing, etc.) may define its own evaluation formula or ROI model, hurting credibility and scalability.

- *Inability to build conversion criteria or attribution models*

Let's admit it: The lack of transparency in the media sector (not just digital), helped build a very tall wall that blocks marketers from determining attribution or lead conversion models. Many "magic" black boxes have been created, new terms invented, and unintelligible indicators used in a way that confuses users and deceives decision-makers. Most organizations have not yet evolved the idea of building their own attribution models.

Marketers must understand that, in order for marketing to become strategic to the business, they must redefine KPIs. Impressions, reach, views, and clicks are the equivalent of the old-timers' GRP, OTS, etc. You cannot pay salaries with them! All these less-demanding metrics are accepted in part because the very same channels in which you market are setting the evaluation standard. First-click, last-click, time decay – all are attribution models based on who knows what. They are completely removed from the business, and CEOs don't even care to see them. The smoke and mirrors they represent – complete with complicated names, impossible-to-understand acronyms, secret algorithms, and black boxes – have never been accepted in the real business environment. This is despite many marketers' efforts to impose them as the measurement standard. Current attribution models lack an unbiased observation and are based on "secret algorithms" that are the same for yogurt as they are for insurance. They also lack isolation criteria that would help organizations figure the actual influence of each touch point in their customers' decision-making process.

The good news is that you can build conversion criteria and attribution models that connect marketing and sales projects with real economic impact. The bad news is that you will never be able to buy such a model off the shelf – you have to build it yourself.

- *Evaluation is often done as a post-project activity*

When evaluation is done as an add-on process, it loses its capability to deliver measurable business results. Measurement and evaluation of sales and marketing projects and campaigns should be part of each project's or each campaign's planning and architecture. Objectives must be defined from inception; data collection and the entire project should be planned from the ROI/business perspective as much as from the communications point of view. Think of it like going for a run: You can't simply run until you get tired and then try to figure out how far and for how long the run was, unless you planned ahead to bring a pedometer with you or turned the GPS of your mobile on. Similarly, it will be very hard to measure the economic return on sales and/or marketing activities if you did not plan to do so in advance.

- *Lack of knowledge about how to link marketing and sales inputs to outputs that have an impact on the business bottom line*

The key to ROI is to be able to translate all sales and marketing inputs into monetary outputs – meaning that with time, resources, and a sound methodology (like the ROI Marketing Matrix), managers will be able to connect what they do on the communications level (including intangibles) to economic impact in most cases. For the purpose of linking results to business impact, it is necessary to know how to manage statistics, mathematical models, and business-related variables, such as net and gross profit margins, customer lifetime value, etc. But you don't need to be a mathematician. The use of statistical models is confusing and difficult to absorb for most practitioners. Statistical precision is needed when high-impact/strategic variables are measured, but in many cases, simple statistics and calculations are all that are needed, and in most cases, they are readily available online or as part of standard spreadsheet formulas.

- *Failure to see the medium/long-term payoff of evaluation*

Not knowing whether you are ill doesn't make you healthy. In the same way, not knowing whether your project loses money does not prevent it from losing it. Sooner or later, somebody will have to pay the bill. When thinking about economic returns, managers should not be afraid of negative results; it would be much worse not to know about them and to keep losing money throughout the years. ROI Marketing allows marketing and sales departments to align with, and show, their contribution to business objectives, linking those contributions to a budget (therefore transforming marketing and sales activities into an investment). It also creates benchmarks for future projects, solid support for projects that work, and a clear picture of those that don't. This, in turn, makes it easier to change processes and/or to eliminate them, contributing again to the health of the business. Clearly showing this contribution (whether negative or positive) can only speak well of marketers' professional skills and attitudes as members of the organization. Of course, if the results are negative, the marketer (always thinking as a contributor to the company) should bring ideas and initiatives to turn these results into positive ones – or bring alternative projects that should have a positive return instead.

- *Inability to transform business intelligence into operations*

Since ROI calculation is not standardized and credibility is low, most businesses do not transform the business intelligence generated by their findings and evaluation cycles into working processes and procedures. This way, the analysis or return stays in the world of theory and becomes almost futile knowledge.

- *Lack of support from key stakeholders*

Important internal customers sometimes fail to give the support needed to ensure success. Practicing ROI Marketing means involving not only the company's communications tools and resources, but also all other departments that can become sources of information, stakeholders, and/or beneficiaries of the information. Executive or management support is required to guarantee implementation success. ROI Marketing practices close the gap so often encountered between sales and marketing departments, bringing them closer and allowing them to work together with a common aim.

Summary bullets:

- Plan and work to achieve business results through marketing rather than to simply execute marketing plans.

- The purpose, source, timing, and objectives of measurements should be thoroughly considered as part of the project-planning phase and prior to any execution.

- There is a planning phase and an execution phase on your way to ROI Marketing.

- Identify barriers and limitations; plan and work to overcome them.

- Identify enablers and leverage them throughout the process.

- Use technology with the aim to collect data and measure but also to achieve results.

Chapter III:
The ROI Marketing Matrix:
The Theory Behind It

How Was It Created?

In December of 1997, a friend of mine, Karlheinz K. (still one of my best friends after all these years) and I created Karpa Marketing & Events Inc. in the United States. Three years later, we were operating in Europe as an integrated marketing agency. In a very fragmented market, we (like everybody else, big or small, multinational or independent) struggled to stand out and make our offer worth potential clients' money. At that time, we decided that we needed to do something different and came up with the idea of having a variable compensation model for our clients. We offered clients the option to work under a pricing model based on the results of the marketing projects we implemented on their behalf. Our fees were tied to key performance indicators related to the interactions and impressions generated by our projects and campaigns: reach, attendance, registrations, leads, redemption, etc. If we surpassed the objectives, we would make more money; if we didn't reach them, we would make less.

We did not realize it then, but that was the first milestone in the development of ROI Marketing Matrix as it exists today. The first step in this direction was forcing ourselves (and our clients) to think in terms of quantitative objectives.

It didn't take long to realize that we were not the only company doing this. We then decided to push the limits and offer our clients a variable compensation model based on sales. If our clients sold above objectives based on the marketing activities we executed, we would make more money. If they sold less than the set objectives, we would make less. This was a risky proposition for us, but it turned out to be a very profitable one. The problem was that we were making money, but our clients weren't. Their sales volume was up, but the sales weren't profitable.

This was the second relevant milestone for the ROI Marketing Matrix, as we (and our clients) were forced to think in terms of profit, rather than in terms of sales volume. This is how the first version of the ROI Marketing methodology was born. It has been perfected through practice during the last 10 years.

As you can see, the ROI Marketing Matrix is not a methodology that appeared on a drawing board as a result of pure theory. It evolved from practice. It was originally a set of steps, which became processes and procedures, which then translated into a systematic approach that is today a solid, robust methodology.

Introduction to the ROI Marketing Matrix

The ROI Marketing Matrix has two well-defined phases:

- The planning phase: *ROI Marketing Cascade*
- The execution phase: *ROI Marketing Ladder*

The planning phase deploys the ROI Marketing Cascade, which walks you from business alignment to ROI validation of the project and/or campaign, and lays out predictive modelling to anticipate possible outcomes (called an ROI Sensitivity Analysis). This phase ensures that once the sales or marketing project starts, managers not only work on execution, but also on measurement as part of the process. This phase happens prior to any investment.

The execution phase uses the ROI Marketing Ladder. It starts with the investment and evolves from getting in contact with the market through reporting to the correspondent stakeholder (boss, shareholder, board, etc.). With the ROI Marketing Ladder, we will work our way up by collecting data, relating the communications world to the business world, showing marketing's contribution in real economic terms, and providing milestones that will boost sales and marketing in a continuous improvement process.

The ROI Marketing Matrix works under the assumption that the goal is to determine the economic return of sales and marketing projects and/or campaigns. It uses two levels of evaluation: market and business. And it uses six dimensions of measurement: positioning messages, education messages, interactions, costs, revenues, and return.

Everything that is measured in the first level of evaluation – at the market level – in any dimension (messages and/or interactions) should relate to the second level of evaluation – at the business level – and its dimensions (cost, revenues, and, eventually, return) in a direct, unequivocal, and accepted way. The levels and dimensions translate into a chain of impact, as shown in the next graphic.

Chart 1: ROI Marketing Matrix Framework – Evaluation Levels & Measurement Dimensions

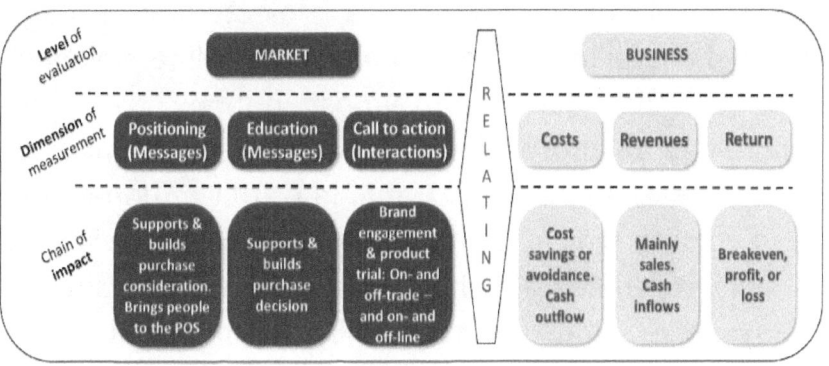

In order to evaluate the actual economic outcome of any sales and/or marketing project, it is necessary to generate a link between what is executed at the market level and the impact it has on the business level. This link is called the *relating factor* in the methodology. For instance, if we want to increase sales, we should be able to show – in a reliable, credible, and accepted way – the relationship between the messages and interactions we delivered to, and generated with, clients and/or consumers, and the actual variation in sales that can be attributed to the influence of those messages and interactions.

The ROI Marketing Matrix expresses this need and helps establish objectives for each of the different dimensions of measurement. Each of these measurement dimensions can also be broken down into subparts, depending on the overall expected impact of the campaign or project.

What are the typical key performance indicators (KPIs) that can help to define the objectives in each dimension? Marketing and sales projects have a huge variety of useful indicators, from on- to off-line, below or above the line (although almost nobody uses this terminology anymore), numeric distribution (number of points of sale), on- and off-trade, in or out of home, etc. This diversity, which can sometimes add complexity to the evaluation, can also help managers identify several performance indicators that will aid in defining the objectives.

The table on page 80 shows some of the most typical indicators used in marketing and sales projects. The sources of relevant data are also vast. In sales and marketing, in contact with the market, using point-of-sale, digital media, and mobile technologies, it would be almost impossible not to be able to find or define indicators and collect relevant information about them.

Table 2: Key Performance Indicators

Level	Dimension	Common Performance Indicators
Market	Positioning	o Awareness o Reputation o Target alignment
Market	Education	o Degree of knowledge o Demonstrated skills o Correct vs. incorrect use
Market	Off-trade Interactions	o Attendance o Product test o Events
Market	On-trade Interactions	o Point-of-sale materials o Promotions o On-site registration o Sampling
Market	Online Interactions	o Social media o Web o Mobile
Market	Off-line Interactions	o Direct marketing o Sponsorships o Product demos
Business	Cost	o Marketing expenditures o Fines o Returns
Business	Revenues	o Sales o Donations
Business	Return	o Rate of return o Customer lifetime value o Cost-benefit ratio

Levels of Evaluation & Measurement Dimensions

1. Market

The first level of evaluation is "market." Also known as "touchpoints" in marketing, it refers to the actual contact with clients, consumers, prospects, and/or those who will generate or influence the behaviors that will eventually lead to an actual sales transaction. From the ROI marketing perspective, this level has three measurement dimensions:

1. Positioning (messages): This entails the deployment of messages through any sort of media, aiming to influence or determine the place, image, or idea the consumer, client, or prospect has in his or her mind about a given product, service, and/or brand. It is linked to the intangibles and the way members of the target audience feel and/or think in each personal relationship with the brand.

2. Education (messages): This encompasses messages aiming to transfer specific knowledge to the target audience. These could refer to product availability, colors, and sizes, place to buy, price, and generally everything the target should know about accessing and/or acquiring and/or using the product or service: offers, new launches, etc.

3. Call to action: Although these activities usually start with the delivery of a message, their aim is to generate an interaction, persuading people to take a given action (redemption, registration, visit, sample, etc.) that will be measured. It relates to behaviors rather than to images or knowledge. Interactions happen in one or a combination of the following environments:

   a. *Off-trade*: These initiatives happen outside of the point of sale. They are mostly related to bringing traffic to the point of sale, creating a brand experience, and/or generating a first contact with the brand, product, or service. Examples: events, sponsorship, direct-mail sampling, etc.
   b. *On-trade*: These initiatives happen at the point of sale. It is known that the biggest part of most purchasing decisions in fast-moving consumer goods happens at the point of sale. Examples: dealer test drives, supermarket samplings, digital channels, etc.
   c. *Off-line*: Communications in a non-digital environment. Examples: billboards, direct marketing, point-of-sale materials, etc.
   d. *Online*: Communications in a digital environment. Examples: web, social

media, mobile communications devices, etc.

2. Business

The second level of evaluation is "business." In this case, some hard data unequivocally have an impact on business and can be measured in three dimensions:

1. *Cost savings and avoidance:* These include, but are not limited to, cost per acquisition (if segmentation is improved, for instance, the cost per acquisition could be reduced), presence at point of sale, reduced churn rates, diminished return rates, customer complaints, warranty claims, and better procurement. All could lead to cost savings. In addition, improved project planning can help to avoid fines and fees, etc.

2. *Revenues:* It is clear that one of the main purposes of all sales and marketing projects is usually to increase profitable sales. For the purpose of the ROI Marketing model, we will consider revenues (or gross revenues), as all cash inflows originating mostly from sales.

3. *Returns:* Reducing costs or increasing sales will not benefit the business if it is not done profitably. Returns refers to the difference between costs and revenues. A project will be profitable if revenues are higher than costs; if costs are higher, it will be unprofitable.

The ROI Marketing Matrix Phases

An ROI evaluation should never be considered a post-execution analysis tool. Attempting to measure the return of a project once the project has been executed is generally a futile exercise. In the best cases, the evaluation will be based on broad assumptions and estimations that will be disputable, with questionable credibility. That is why the ROI Marketing management model described in the ROI Marketing Matrix is based on both of these phases: planning and execution.

The planning phase is known as the ROI Marketing Cascade and the execution phase as the ROI Marketing Ladder. Investing in the project starts the execution phase; each of the phases includes four steps, as shown in the following graphic:

Chart 2: ROI Marketing Phases

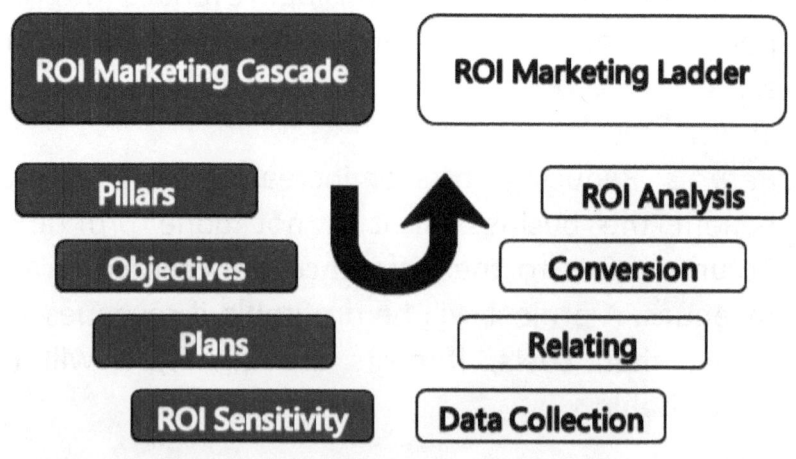

ROI Marketing Matrix Phase 1: The ROI Marketing Cascade

The ROI Marketing Cascade represents the planning phase of the methodology. This is a crucial phase, as it will determine the steps to take in order to be able to measure the actual profitability of sales and marketing projects during and after execution. It entails preparation (objective setting and alignment), validation, prediction, and decision-making. The final outcome of this stage can be split in two: go-no-go decision-making and a kickoff plan that will allow you to measure ROI while executing and after the project.

As previously mentioned, ROI evaluation is not a post-execution analysis. It is a process that starts from the very beginning of (or even before) the planning process, as soon as an organization decides to start planning a project or campaign. The main reason to start the ROI evaluation work even before planning is that the project must be aligned with the rest of the organization: its mission and vision, its sales and marketing plans, and any other compliance issues (legal, practices, cultural, etc.). This first stage in the planning process is called "The Pillars."

1. ROI Marketing Cascade: The Pillars
The pillars are the fundamentals of any business. They are the core elements of the overall strategy and the

foundations of all business practices, processes, and procedures.

This means that we should see marketing and sales activities from a broader scope in their alignment with, and impact on, the overall vision and mission of the business, its objectives, and its global strategy. It calls for an approach that goes beyond, and starts before, any sales and/or marketing activities. This alignment should be present and seen in all contacts: internal, with suppliers, with clients and consumers, and with all stakeholders at large.

Each department in any organization should have a clear set of principles that will help them to assess whether their work is "aligned" or "not aligned" with the business core. A profitable sales or marketing plan will be of little help if it is not growing around the organization's guiding principles and scope in such a way that it establishes a symbiotic relationship with them.

In this ever-changing market, with rapid movements in consumer behavior, it is imperative that marketers, sales people, and really everybody within the organization have an overall vision of how what they do affects the business – not only economically but also socially and environmentally. It is known that the nature of any business goes way beyond profit. It is mandatory that there is awareness, alignment, and compliance with principles that transcend profit.

The whole world is changing in all senses. The messages we used to deliver through conventional media (TV, press, and radio) are moving to their digital versions. Digital media is being transformed by the way society interacts with and through social media, and social media is more and more often accessed on mobile devices by consumers on the move. It is increasingly difficult to predict what consumers will do and the way they will influence corporate plans, but we all know they do and they will keep doing so. The consistency of companies' marketing and sales plans with their philosophies, scopes, missions, and visions, regardless of media, channel, or activity carried, is essential to establishing a clear, durable, and positive relationship with diverse audiences and markets, wherever they are, whatever they do, and however they communicate.

In short, The Pillars stage entails, at a minimum, aligning each project with the mission and vision of the organization, as well as with the marketing and sales overall plans.

If the sales and marketing strategy is aligned with the business, the next step is to make sure the right project plan is in place, and that begins with setting the right objectives. This is the second stage for the ROI Marketing Cascade (the planning phase).

CASE I: ROI Marketing Cascade – About Alignment with the Pillars

Industry: Energy Generation
Type of organization: Multinational company (Spain)
Offering: B2B

Introduction:
Few marketing departments have a more complicated task than the ones dealing with energy generation. Clients are large, often public organizations with highly regulated prices and end users who are linked to their client – not for economic reasons, but as part of a political system. These companies need to comply with strict and imposed market regulation. They must please and/or partner with energy distributors, transportation companies, and a large series of stakeholders that range from investors, banks, analysts, and media, to political and governmental organizations, universities, associations, NGOs, and more. In this scenario, both what the company does and how it does it are very relevant. The mission and vision of an energy-generation company must deal not only with business results, but also with the social and environmental impact of what it does. The monetary value or impact on the economics of the business, in this case, is directly influenced by the perceived alignment between the company's objectives and the expectations of both stakeholders and society at large, regarding those issues that impact either of them directly (company valuation, environmental impact,

contribution to education, etc.). That is what this case is about.

The company's goal:
To find a way to show the economic value and impact of its stakeholder management program.

How did they achieve it?
By surveying all stakeholders and extracting business intelligence from their expectations and perceptions about company performance. In addition, the survey generated information about the degree of influence that intangibles have on business-related decision-making processes, linking soft issues to business performance and defining its own attribution model.

What was the result?
The company started a completely new way of managing stakeholders, with lines of action that included, but were not limited to, internal organization (people and departments, as well as governance bodies), a new strategic approach to communications (internal and external), new tools to manage information, a completely new set of rules of engagement, and a monitoring system. A larger budget was assigned to the project, which started to plan an international deployment.

Conclusions:
The alignment between the pillars of the company and the expectations of the society it impacts is fundamental

for the business long term and to support its business cycle. If societal expectations shift during a sustained period of time, pillars (including mission and vision) must adjust to it. For the stakeholder management program to be sustainable, it needs to generate value for both the company and its stakeholders. Stakeholder management improves ratings and indices (such as the Dow Jones Sustainability Index, for instance) that improve the share value, directly impacting the bottom line of the business.

2. ROI Marketing Cascade: Objectives

If you carefully read the marketing project briefs or plans you receive from your clients (if you are working in an agency) or the ones you and your colleagues write for agencies, you will notice that briefing memos mostly state an intention, what the authors would like to do. For instance: "We would like to have a loyalty program," "do a direct marketing campaign," "a discount package," "a retention promotion," etc. But, make no mistake, these are not objectives. They are intentions. These intentions cannot be measured. Under these scenarios, the reasons why a project might have been successful depend on subjective, or not terribly rigorous, criteria.

The following list shows real "objectives" I have read in marketing plans, from real companies I have encountered over the years:

- To unlock "x product line" market, increasing share by six points.
- To increase brand awareness.
- To become a reliability partner for "segment A."
- To improve market coverage (increase visibility from 10% to 50%).
- To develop attractive service offers (total cost of ownership).
- To develop an education program.

Do any of them sound familiar to you? If you read these objectives carefully, you will soon notice that in most cases (not all of them), it will be difficult to determine, after execution, whether the project was successful or not. In some cases, they set a broad goal with no boundaries (How would you know if you became a "reliability partner"?). In others (for instance, "To develop an education program"), they state what the manager would like to do, rather than the actual purpose (What do we want an education program for?).

Marketing and sales activities are all means to reach a goal, not a purpose. Marketing and sales project planning should focus on the objectives to reach, rather than on the activities to execute. However, even in its broadest expression, I've never seen a brief that said, "we would like to make money with this project," "we would like to achieve a positive ROI with this investment," or "the project should pay for itself" as an objective. While these also are not proper objectives, at least they state a business-related goal, rather than an intention to conduct an activity.

Of course, many briefings list "to increase sales" as an objective (curiously, most of the time as the last objective). But is it really an objective stated this way, or is it a nice-to-have or must-have phrase that we know the boss wants to see in our plans?

This does not mean that managers can forget about execution or shouldn't have a say regarding what could work best to achieve their objectives. After all, sales and marketing managers are the ones who have the experience with the brand, the products, and the services, and control the touch points with the target groups and markets. But, in order to measure the economic impact of sales and marketing projects, during the planning process it is vital to consider all the more typical variables, as well as all of those that will help you to evaluate the project from an economic perspective (costs, revenues, and returns), and that impact the business bottom line.

The ROI Marketing Matrix suggests setting objectives at the chain-of-impact level, from the market and business levels of evaluation, at the different dimensions of measurement: positioning, education, interaction, costs, revenues, and, eventually, return.

The market level of evaluation (we could also call this "communication" in its broadest sense) is about sales and marketing as usual. At this level, managers think about delivering messages that aim to take a position in the mind of customers, to teach something to different market segments, and/or to establish interactions with them (participation, registration, redemption, sampling, tests, etc.) that will ultimately lead to an increase in sales. But this doesn't mean that you will be able to measure the contribution of the project to the business, even if you somehow manage to relate a certain increase in sales to the project or campaign.

As comedian Groucho Marx might say, "If you don't know where you are going, you may end up anywhere." The way we define where we want to go in sales and marketing is, while in alignment with the business mission, vision, and strategy, by setting proper and measurable objectives for each and every project at each dimension of measurement.

Objectives should be clearly stated, achievable, and measurable. Most of the time, objectives are defined as a set of intentions that claim certain results as their own, based on inference from project inputs or correlations. For instance, if the objective was that "we should increase awareness" about a new product, we inferred that by having "x" number of unique visitors to our website, we managed to develop such awareness. But is this the right conclusion to draw? Shouldn't we verify, somehow, that such awareness was certainly developed? And what does awareness mean, exactly?

In the ROI Marketing Matrix, you should set objectives for every project on each of the measurement dimensions: messages (positioning and education), interactions, costs, and revenues. Eventually, you will also be able to add return as a dimension of evaluation.

Many people believe that measuring the economic return (ROI) on sales and marketing is not possible, but as the philosopher Ernst Cassirer would say: "We can hardly blame science just because we've asked the wrong questions." Without clear, measurable objectives, there's no way we can start our quest for sales and marketing accountability and everything that such accountability entails. Objectives are the cornerstone of sales and marketing plans and will set the clear and unbiased line between failure and success.

- Requirements for objectives:

In order for objectives to be useful to the evaluation purpose, the ROI Marketing Matrix suggests that they have three key elements, known as "TIQ Elements":

*T*ime-framed

All objectives should have a measurement-final milestone. In the case of sales and marketing projects, this milestone is set by the length of time we consider our project may have an impact for – the "period of influence" we will refer to a bit later. For instance, when measuring the impact of a trade show booth on corporate communications and business, how long does the manager think the trade show's impact or influence will last? It is advisable that this period of time is agreed to by the main stakeholders or evaluating body so it is accepted from the very beginning. In most cases, this period of influence will go beyond the execution period of the project. It is discretional, and it must be agreed upon among the stakeholders.

*I*ndicator (measurable)

All objectives should be measurable and quantifiable. What are the variables that we should be measuring to have an impact on business and communications? These variables could be financial measures, such as costs, revenues, and profits, or they could be variables that are related to the core and scope of the business, such as carbon dioxide footprint, social impact, etc. They could also be the usual marketing performance indicators, such as visitors to a website, registrations, samples tested, downloads, clicks, etc. They are the performance indicators to be measured during the evaluation cycle that are directly related or will later be linked to the business bottom line. An indicator must be measurable. If it cannot be counted, it cannot serve as an indicator. But, remember this adage: "Not everything that can be counted counts."

Quantity (achievable)

Quantity is represented by the threshold that marks the unequivocal difference between having achieved the objective or not. It represents the objective countable frontier. It may seem like common sense, but frequently, managers overlook this *sine qua non* characteristic of any objective: achievability. Achievability (or lack thereof) will become evident during project or campaign planning and be completely confirmed with the ROI Sensitivity Analysis (explained ahead), which should be carried out prior to the execution phase.

"An objective without a plan is a dream."

CASE II: ROI Marketing Cascade – About Setting Objectives

Industry: Healthcare
Type of organization: Multinational company (Holland)
Offering: B2B and B2C

Introduction:
Setting objectives seems like a rather easy task, but taking a closer look and aiming to make those objectives actionable and measurable (let alone achievable) is a more daunting job. This was the case at this company that was used to setting objectives in such a way that they were not measurable, and therefore, although actionable (because they expressed sales and communications intentions), they were useless for monitoring results or establishing a non-biased threshold of success.

Here are some of the real objectives the company had:

- To select three key opinion leaders to support paper publishing and start word-of-mouth advertising.
- To develop an education program to certify sales channel and application.
- To increase sales.
- To improve our relationship with our distribution network.
- To increase media exposure.

The company's goal:
To set these objectives in a measurable way. To standardize the way the company would set future objectives, establishing common performance indicators for all business units. To set an objective way of defining success that depends on actual performance, rather than on reporting level (up and down) perception.

How did they achieve it?
They used the ROI Marketing Matrix dimensions of measurement (positioning, education, interactions, costs, revenues, and return) as the common performance indicators for all business units. They adopted the TIQ Elements (time frame, indicator, and quantity threshold) as required criteria for all objectives.

What was the result?
From then on, all objectives became measurable, each with a clear threshold that marked the frontier between having achieved the objective or not in a non-biased way. Business units had common performance indicators that became known to the other units, aligning them and helping to generate collaboration between departments.

Objectives were rephrased as follows:

Table 3: Old vs. New Objectives

Old Objectives	New Objectives
To select three key opinion leaders (KOL) to support paper publishing and start word-of-mouth advertising.	To select at least three KOL who will endorse paper publishing publicly by gaining exposure in at least two media for each KOL in the next six months after starting the campaign. In the case of digital media, media exposure shall generate engagement of at least 10 comments/likes/forwards per KOL during the same period.
To develop an education program to certify sales channel and application.	To develop a certification program that trains at least 50% of distributors' sales forces in at least 75% of the distribution network during the current year. Certification shall include proof of application in the field/market and correct use of treatment shall be achieved in at least 90% of the cases by the end of this year.
To increase sales.	To influence, in at least 25% of sales, decision-making that leads to an overall sales increase of 15% for the current year.

To improve our relationship with our distribution network.	To be rated as four or above on a scale of five in the overall relationship with our distribution network by the end of the third quarter of the current year.
To increase media exposure.	To increase media exposure value by at least 25% compared to the same period of last year during the quarter after the launch of the new product.

Notice that the first column's statements ("Old Objectives") are not really objectives, but intentions. They cannot be verified, and the degree of achievement will be discretionary, determined by the person marketing is reporting to. It will be subjective, and it could be that the person receiving the report might not consider any growth of sales that might have happened as sufficient. By the time you find that out, it will be too late. The statement "to increase media exposure," for instance, is missing a period of influence (time reference) and a threshold quantity. When should that increase in sales happen to be considered achieved? How much additional sales must be achieved to consider the project successful? In contrast, the statements on the right ("New Objectives") contain all the necessary elements to be considered objectives. They can all be measured, and the criteria to determine whether they were achieved or not cannot be biased. That's why it is so important to reach consensus about your objectives (as well as about things like relating factors and monetization criteria) prior to starting the project – it helps take away all subjectivity around the definition of success.

Conclusions:
Setting proper objectives makes a company's activities operational and allows them to have a measured impact. Without them, departments tend to work their own way, independently and in silos. Sharing information does not weaken the person or department, it empowers them with strategically higher and measurable impact! Success can be determined objectively.

3. ROI Marketing Cascade: Plans

Project planning from the ROI Marketing perspective is not much different from what managers are used to doing, generally speaking. It just requires a broader perspective and scope, understanding that what you are looking for goes beyond the usual performance indicators to the bottom line of the business. What are the main requirements of project planning within the ROI Marketing Matrix?

- Planning should *focus on results delivery*, rather than on execution. Begin with the end in mind.

- *Never lose sight of the objectives.* Always ask: How is this task, activity, action, event, advertising, direct marketing, etc., going to contribute to achieving any of the objectives? Objectives are the starting point of your Data Collection Plan.

- Plan how you are going to *establish a cause-effect relationship* between the standard marketing and sales performance indicators (messages and interactions) and the business objectives (costs, revenues, and returns) at stake. *Validate* that relation with the person you are reporting to. Is it acceptable, reliable, and believable?

- Think about how you will *gather specific information* regarding the KPIs that will demonstrate that you have achieved the objectives. This is where you should use the what, when, who, and how checklist (3WH checklist) explained ahead.

- Plan also on what basis you will *give a monetary value* (a measure of revenue and return) to each of the KPIs measured. *Validate* such criteria with the person you are reporting to. Is it acceptable, reliable, and believable?

- Start defining and controlling the *costs involved and impacted* by your project or campaign. Make sure you count all costs and avoid double accounting.

- *Validate for commercial viability and establish predictive models* before execution by using the ROI Sensitivity Analysis. What are the chances this project and/or campaign might be economically successful? Is it commercially sound?

Once your project has been aligned with the pillars and measurable objectives are properly set, it is necessary to plan for three activities that address the following questions:

   a. How will we establish a direct cause-effect relationship between what the project is doing and the inputs of money it generates? The way to find the answer to this question is by using RELATING FACTORS.

b. How will we collect the information needed to prove it? The answer to this question is your DATA COLLECTION PLAN.

c. How will we convert those inputs into returns for the business? The answer to this question is achieved by using MONETARY CONVERSION criteria.

- **Relating Factors Plan**

At this point, we reach a critical stage in measuring the economic impact of sales and marketing investments, its Achilles heel, the threshold of its robustness, and hence of its credibility: the relating factors. These are the factors that connect your marketing or sales plan with actual purchases.

Defining the relating factors is one of the key elements to building a robust system of measurement that will generate overall credibility (one of the weak points of most ROI evaluations). The relating factors will be used to attribute economic results to the performance of messages and interactions. Relating factors are usually known as "attribution models" in marketing, or "isolation criteria" in other cases. In marketing, these relating factors have one peculiarity: they need to isolate two marketing-specific characteristics for economic transactions.

In most industries, there is usually a direct cause-effect relationship between input and output. For instance, when buying a machine to fully produce one product, companies know that 100% of products coming out of that machine have been produced by it, and that 100% of each product has also been produced by the same machine. In marketing, however, it is necessary to determine how many purchases the project being analyzed has impacted, and what the influence of that project was on each of those purchases. In other words, not all sales can be attributed to my marketing and/or sales project, and for each sale impacted by my project, not all benefits can be credited to that given project – only part of them. The criteria to relate communications to business must follow a standard:

- *Be simple*: Everybody should understand the criteria across the organization, and at all levels (C-level executives, managers, etc.).
- *Be robust*: The way criteria assign value should be rigorous, conservative, and relevant.
- *Be reliable*: The sources of information should be verified, and the statistics corrected for margin of error and confidence interval; the scenarios or possible assumptions should also be based on relevant and significant samples.
- *Be accepted*: If the criteria have not previously been accepted, chances are that during the report presentation, managers will end up discussing the methodology rather than the results of the project or campaign.

Defining the relating factors should answer the following two questions:

1. How many purchases has my project impacted?
2. What was the influence of my project on each purchasing act?

The answer to the first question can be found more accurately and unquestionably. The answer to the second one is within the mind of the buyer, and therefore a bit more complex to define in a robust way. But it is not impossible!

Remember, relating means finding the cause-effect relationship between the inputs generated by the messages and interactions (market level) and their impact on the costs and revenues (business level). This relationship has to be unequivocal, to the best extent possible. Analysts should base their calculations on certain connections and/or on accepted estimations. There are several possible ways in which managers can generate these correlations when planning to build them in advance. But caution should be exercised, as correlation does not necessarily mean causation. That is why planning to measure ROI is so important; it will most likely not be possible to establish these cause-effect relationships as a post-execution quest, and the overall credibility of the evaluation depends in large part on these relating factors.

If you do not generate a robust attribution model for total purchases impacted by the project and the influence of the project on each purchasing act, your evaluation will be reduced to the communication or market level. It will then have limited connection to the business. In other words, the CEO will not believe in the results you are presenting, or, in the best scenario, will decide the results have limited strategical relevance to P&L (one of the CEO's main concerns). Marketing budgets will continue to be treated as a cost.

The already-famous and often-misused "customer journey" helps us to define the different stages consumers and clients go through until the actual purchase decision is made and executed. The customer journey has different paths, even for the same product in the very same market. Consumers embrace new media with new devices at an ever-faster pace, making it difficult to segment by type of media or channel (social, web, store, etc.). "Omni-channel" has been the name of the game for some time already, and defining the path through those channels to create segments is rather difficult (if not impossible). So, the customer journey acquires more relevance. Not being able to segment by channel and/or media, marketers must be able to identify "when" each consumer is in each stage of the journey towards purchase in order to define objectives, plan actions, and monitor results. Furthermore, if marketers and salespeople understand in which part of the journey each client or consumer is, it will be possible to model attribution, which is paramount to defining marketing and sales efforts' contribution to the business variables and, ultimately, the actual return of each media and/or channel.

Attribution is easy to endorse but hard to implement. Digital media have already tried several arbitrary criteria (last click, linear distribution, time decay, etc.) that, while defining the attribution, were not robust enough to generate credibility for decision-makers. Other models were and are constantly being developed by media, channels, or platform providers, but your best bet is to define your own attribution model and work with your providers to implement it in whatever IT system they offer to you.

Initial attribution models only consider the impact of a tool on sales whenever that tool was identified as a touch point in the customer journey. Although this might be accurate, it is not exhaustive. Isolating the number of purchases impacted by a marketing project is not enough. It is necessary to isolate the influence of each touch point on the final decision-making process, in a way that not only determines the customer's "path" but also the relevance of each "step" on this path.

It is accepted that the customer journey has some common defined moments:

Consideration:
The initial moment when the customer or consumer is thinking about buying something. In his or her mind, it

starts with a question: "Where would I get this?" or "Who does it?" The radar starts scanning for options, and your company or product had better become a blip on that radar screen, or else you have already lost more than half of the battle. If you happen to be on the customer's path with a touch point at this moment, you will be way ahead of many competitors. If you are already on the radar screen, it means that you conducted good marketing in the past. Positioning is key at this point, because you need potential clients to think of you. At this stage, brand awareness, reputation, and a variety of intangibles can lead the way onto the consideration path. At the end of this moment, the customer will end up with a set of options ready for the next step: assessment.

Assessment:
At this moment, the client has already decided to buy and is actively choosing the best option. Gathering specific information is key at this stage. Newcomers (missed during the consideration moment) can arise at this stage, so never give up your battle for lost. (By the way, most marketers prefer to invest at this phase because it is more influential than the consideration one and consumers stay open to new options.) Education and interactions are key in this moment, since consumers need to know and understand several things about the product and/or services they are about to buy, and the way they interact with the product and sales channel may become determinant (sampling, test drive, customer service, social media,

etc.). During the evaluation, there will be dropouts and selected options that will move into the next moment: purchasing.

Purchasing:
Some people may be led to believe that this is the end of the customer journey, but nothing could be further from the truth. How many times have you gone to the supermarket thinking about buying something that you have considered and ended up with a competitor's product? Of course, this is more relevant to fast-moving consumer goods than to more complex purchases (a car, for instance), but the interaction at the point of purchase can turn the whole decision-making process in another direction. Furthermore, the whole experience of buying (even if concluded) can become input for future buying, recommendations, social media interactions, reputation, etc. Purchasing triggers the next step: experience.

Experience:
Experience refers to the interactions the client has after actually buying the product and/or service. It is the initial act of brand expansion and loyalty loop, and it will determine new cycles of consideration and evaluation for future purchases. It is definitely a key element of your marketing mix if you want to increase sales, maximizing profits and minimizing risks. Through the experience, you will be building the Holy

Grail of marketing and sales, which is the next step: loyalty.

Loyalty:
A loyal customer is one who will skip consideration and will do a much more selective evaluation based on your offer as a model to beat. You have the upper hand of competitive engagement. Your competitors will have to look up to you and try to improve on your offer. Your acquisition costs will be much lower (increasing your profits) and you will be in a much better position to increase repeat sales and cross-selling.

Each one of these moments requires touch points. To be able to measure how many purchases were impacted by a project, you must build attribution models that clearly and unequivocally define the split between buyers who were impacted by the project and buyers who, under the same conditions, were not impacted. You must determine, for each purchasing act, which touch points entered each moment (which is what most attribution models are doing nowadays). As we will see in the Data Collection Plan description ahead, this can be done via control groups, trend line analysis, and a wide array of tools.

Each one of these moments is also influenced by a series of factors. The way these factors influence each purchase decision is based on several aspects, ranging from the perception of each person about the product or service being considered, to the convenience for the consumer in terms of proximity, price, social recognition, and a long list of other factors. So, the customer journey is not the only thing to consider – you must also consider the factors influencing the decision-making process that are not touch points (price, reputation, word of mouth, etc.). Its complexity does not mean that we cannot measure its influence, and as Peter Drucker would say, "What gets measured, gets improved." The perception of influence of any given factor in the decision-making process responds to the second question: What is the influence of my project on each purchasing act? Measuring this last perception is required in order to complete an ROI evaluation for any sales or marketing project. Otherwise, evaluation will be skewed, because whatever attribution model you use to assign a purchase to a given touch point will be allocating 100% of any variation in sales to that given touch point, which we all know is not accurate.

How can we measure the influence of non-touch-point factors and touch point efficiency in the decision-making process? The answer to this question must value the "importance" of a given feature or characteristic to the customer, showing its relevance and the way it influences preferences as a decision driver for each group of customers and/or consumers. To measure levels of preferences, we can use two approaches: self-explained method and/or conjoint analysis. Self-explained method is a compositional approach, meaning that it starts with the features of a product or service and works all the way up to the complete offering. Conjoint analysis is a de-compositional approach, meaning the complete offer is decomposed into the importance of each feature. There is not general agreement as to which method is better, and you should determine which one to use based on the nature of your product or service. Split sample studies to compare results of the two methods haven't shown conclusive evidence as to which method is best.

Whichever method you use, the way to determine the influence of different features or characteristics on the decision-making process is by asking. The challenge, then, is whom, how, when, and where to ask. This topic is covered ahead in the next needed plan: Data Collection Plan.

The issue of relating factors is, as previously mentioned, crucial for the overall robustness of the evaluation and fundamental to building credibility.

CASE III: ROI Marketing Cascade – About Generating Relating Factors

Industry: Energy Management and Automation
Type of organization: Multinational organization (France)
Offering: B2B and B2C

Introduction:
The market for electric management systems is very close to several other markets (pharmaceutical, for instance). It is highly regulated for safety reasons, with a large and very fragmented multilevel distribution system, a clear prescriber (the decorator, engineer, architect, etc., or the doctor in the case of pharma), established influencers (the contractor, etc., or the pharmacist in the case of pharma). Combining all these factors into a sound and effective sales and marketing plan is a challenge these types of businesses deal with on a regular basis.

The company's goal:
In this case, the client company, a French multinational, organized a series of events for distributors, architects, engineers, and contractors. The intent was to deliver training and product demos, as well as to recruit new leads and improve the company's relationship with its distribution network. The company wanted to understand the impact of those activities on the decision-making process of its clients, prescribers, and

influencers. The main question was how to isolate (determine the relating factor) the effect of each one of the components influencing the decision-making process for each stage.

How did they achieve it?
They key to isolating each of the influences was to figure out whether the attendees learned what they were supposed to learn and to determine the influence of each one of those mentioned activities on any eventual purchase decision-making. The company needed to do so in a way that allowed it to define its own attribution model.

The first question in the Relating Factors Plan is how many purchases were impacted by the project. In this case, the isolation was determined by the nature of the project. Obviously, all purchases by people who attended the event that occurred after the event were impacted by the project. The period of influence of the project was determined to be six months, as that is more or less the company's sales cycle. Hence, all sales that occurred during the six months after the event, to people/companies that attended the event, were considered impacted by the event and susceptible to influence.

The second question in the Relating Factors Plan – what influence did each part of the event exert on each decision – was a bit more complex, but completely answerable. Each attendee had to fill in a questionnaire (in exchange for an incentive) with key information. These questions (among others) helped measure influence:

- What was the influence of an event like the one you are attending on your decision-making process?
- What was the influence of product demos on your decision-making process?
- What was the influence of training on your decision-making process?
- How would you grade your relationship with the company? (On a scale of 1 to 10, with 10 being excellent and 1 really poor.) Note: This question had to be asked twice, once before and once after the event, in order to gauge evolution and influence of the event. It also had to include a control group that did not attend the event, verifying that conditions remained the same for the rest of the market.

In all cases, the data from the questionnaire was broken down by the role of the respondent (engineer, contractor, etc.) and identified who was already part of the company's CRM database and who was a new lead.

What was the result?
The company obtained a total of 1,089 valid responses. Considering that its universe included 14,000 contacts, the responses obtained had a 2.85% margin of error and a confidence level of 95% with 50% response distribution. This was much lower than the 5% margin of

error the company had set as the minimum error threshold.

Being more exhaustive, and aiming for a deeper analysis, managers also calculated a margin of error per city, taking into consideration the size of each market. For the sake of simplicity, we used only the overall margin of error in this case.

This French multinational ended up with a chart like the one below (note: this chart only shows responses to the influence question) for each of the seven cities where the events were held:

Influence	City A	Ratings as a % of the total	Compensated Influence	City B	Ratings as a % of the total	Compensated Influence	City C	Ratings as a % of the total	Compensated Influence
10%	1	0.91%	0.10	2	1.16%	0.20	6	3.33%	0.60
20%	1	0.91%	0.20		0.00%	-	2	1.11%	0.40
30%		0.00%	-	2	1.16%	0.60	2	1.11%	0.60
40%	1	0.91%	0.40	6	3.47%	2.40	6	3.33%	2.40
50%	5	4.55%	2.50	15	8.67%	7.50	16	8.89%	8.00
60%	19	17.27%	11.40	20	11.56%	12.00	27	15.00%	16.20
70%	35	31.82%	24.50	48	27.75%	33.60	54	30.00%	37.80
80%	30	27.27%	24.00	47	27.17%	37.60	35	19.44%	28.00
90%	13	11.82%	11.70	14	8.09%	12.60	16	8.89%	14.40
100%	5	4.55%	5.00	19	10.98%	19.00	16	8.89%	16.00
	110	100.00%	79.80	173	100.00%	125.50	180	100.00%	124.40
Average influence per city			72.55%			72.54%			69.11%
Corrected influence per city (*)			70.48%			70.48%			67.14%

Figure obtained by discounting the initial overall margin of error of 2.85%. This responds to a conservative criterion that increases the conclusions' robustness and credibility.

Conclusions:
By defining the overall influence of the event on the decision-making process, the client company was able to relate the event inputs to business outputs by assigning

that given influence as the attributable part of the margin of each sale impacted by the project. This way, the company answered both questions of the Relating Factors Plan.

- **Data Collection Plan**

As Kevin Brown, senior vice president and head of marketing at Credibly, a Fintech lending platform that provides access to capital for U.S.-based small and medium-sized businesses, said in 2015: "The next frontier for marketing teams is finding cohesive alignment with their data science counterparts ... with predictive analytics driving targeted communication with consumers. Data is the rocket fuel for marketing's future." (Courtesy Forbes.com)

Marketers must define, plan to collect, and analyze data in order to extract business intelligence that will allow them to evaluate the actual economic impact of their marketing project on the business bottom line. This data will also facilitate making wiser and more-accurate decisions when planning for future projects. The right business intelligence will allow marketers to plan in a more business-oriented and results-driven fashion.

ROI Marketing requires the collection of data before, during, and after the execution of sales and marketing projects or campaigns, in order to generate cause-effect relationships that will show the economic contribution of marketing and sales. Therefore, it is important to define all the information needed to demonstrate those relationships. The data should be relevant and collected during the period of influence, using a methodology that guarantees its accuracy and truth to the best extent possible. Usually, the data that is closest to the point of sale (either online or off-line) is the most relevant data. Data can be collected from actual interactions and/or behaviors, statistical/arithmetic quantitative testing, or educated assumptions. These last ones must be validated and tested under different scenarios to ensure integrity and relevance. For this purpose, the ROI Marketing Matrix counts on the following 3WH checklist.

Table 4: 3WH Data Collection Checklist

What	What type of data do I need to collect? In most cases, the answer will be represented by the performance indicators defined in each one of your objectives. For instance, you should ask yourself: Which is the countable indicator that will show whether my client understood how to use my product?
When	When am I going to collect the information? When is the proper moment to ask a question? For instance, if you deliver a question related to a training session, you should request the answers after the session is over and not before. (Believe it or not, this has happened!) You must also establish for how long you should collect information, and the answer is always until the end of the period of influence (described ahead).
Who	Who should I ask for the information? Make sure you ask the right source that has and can give you the information. For instance, you can observe a child to learn about the usability of a toy, but you should ask his/her parent about its safety features.
How	How am I going to retrieve the information – via surveys, count, correlation, etc.? For instance, should you gain information about the number of dogs in a neighborhood by the amount of pet food sold in the area or by a registry of nearby veterinarians? The answer to this also refers to, or depends upon, your choice between the self-explained and conjoint analysis methodologies explained earlier in this chapter.

There are three sets of data to collect:

1. *Marketing performance indicators*: data related to the achievements of communications efforts and execution (positioning, education and call-to-action messages, and interactions)

2. *Cost indicators*: direct expenditures derived from the project, as well as non-fixed, indirect, quantifiable impacts that can later be deducted from the margin

3. *Revenue indicators*: income generated by the marketing project

Determining the period of influence of any sales or marketing project is key to evaluating any type of performance in a credible way. It refers to the period during which the project exerts an influence on the decision-making process of the target impacted by it. It usually goes beyond the execution of the project. For instance, if you are evaluating the economic return of a trade show booth, you will want to consider a period of influence that goes beyond the five days of the trade show. In order to define such a time frame, managers have several tools at hand. Some ways to do so include the following:

> *Internal consensus*: a relevant method, and the one most likely to be accepted, is internal questioning. Experienced people within the company can provide an educated guess about

the potential length of impact of any given sales or marketing project in the business. The salesforce is always in contact with the market and represents the group that can come closest to knowing the true period of impact of a project.

Previous experiences: events, direct marketing, advertising, point-of-sale activations, promotions, and a long list of other tools are used by marketing and sales managers to perform their tasks. In some cases, questionnaires, surveys, and research are carried out, and the results can shed light on the period of influence of a given project.

Industry standards: category associations, industry reports, and market research are some of the potential sources of information about the period of influence of marketing activities.

1. *Collecting Marketing Performance Indicators*

Marketing performance indicators are all the indicators that marketers and agencies have historically measured. In essence, marketing is composed of sets of messages delivered through several media and channels that are expected to drive a behavior – an action or the omission of an action. The way these messages influence the minds of consumers and clients, whether consumers and clients have learned anything from these messages, and what consumers and clients did (or didn't do) after receiving them – all can be accurately measured in different ways and with many trustworthy sources.

These indicators are varied and range from awareness and positioning to intention to purchase, knowledge, attendance, clicks, subscription, redemption, and a long list of others. They will never be measured in monetary terms. This is marketing measurement as we all know it, and how it has always been practiced.

To collect this type of data, marketers can use:

- Market studies
- Focus groups
- Digital tools
- Surveys and questionnaires
- Industry associations' reports
- Their own measurements
- R&D reports
- Benchmarking data
- Simple counting (attendees, registrations, visits, etc.)
- And so on

In the ROI Marketing Matrix model, these indicators should be defined in the positioning, education, and interactions objectives.

2. Collecting Cost Indicators

If you do not know how much a project costs, you will never be able to calculate its return. The cost is the actual investment, from which you are expecting to generate a positive result in economic terms (not only in marketing performance terms). Therefore, it is necessary to have strict control and definition of costs to calculate a credible ROI figure. The information about costs is, in most cases, internal, but it is not always simple to retrieve. What are the costs or types of costs to consider when determining the ROI of a sales and/or marketing project or campaign? Here are some examples of marketing and sales costs, although this list is not exhaustive and changes constantly:

- Web design, programming, hosting, and controlling
- Maintenance of databases for loyalty programs
- Media buys
- Cost of company media (microsite, community management, etc.)
- Production costs (booths, direct marketing, point-of-sale material, catering, venue fees, spot, jingle, etc.)
- Giveaways
- Personnel hired for the project or campaign
- Agency fees
- Discounts
- Samples
- Other project fees, such as legal consultation, insurance, etc.

Most of these costs are controlled and handled by the marketing and sales department. In some cases, other departments may be needed.

To be completely exhaustive, you can also choose any part of fixed costs that can be directly and reliably attributed to a given project (such as marketing personnel, R&D, etc.), which are typically embedded in the cost of goods sold. If you choose to do so, make sure you deduct these costs from the margin calculation to be considered as the monetization factor to avoid "double accounting."

To collect these types of data, marketers can use:

- Their own records
- Procurement department reports
- Corporate financial reports
- Internal consultation
- Industry association reports
- Benchmarking data
- Control of their own expenditures
- ERP
- CRM
- Etc.

There is a second set of costs that marketers should consider, and those are the costs that the marketing project reduces (savings it creates). If, as a consequence of the marketing project, for instance, consumers start using a product in a way that reduces breakage and warranty claims, it implies fewer costs that take away from the bottom line of the business. This cost avoidance will also affect the ROI of the project and should be accounted for.

3. *Collecting Revenue Indicators*

To calculate the actual return of any sales or marketing project, you'll need to convert as many sales and marketing variables as possible into monetary values. This is not an easy task, especially if you are doing it for the first time and don't have past projects for reference. However, if you don't count money, you can't determine ROI. You could settle for less, stay at the communications level when measuring impact (as is commonly done), and show the results of a campaign in terms of its impact on awareness, purchase intentions, impressions, etc. In some cases, you may do so. The cost of monitoring and measuring, and its impact on the overall project, will determine whether it is worth measuring the project from an economic point of view.

As I previously mentioned, by defining the relating factors, you should answer the following questions:
1. How many purchases has my project impacted?
2. What was the influence of my project on each purchasing act?

Your plan to collect revenue indicators must be determined by the answers to those two questions and the attribution model you defined in the Relating Factors Plan.

Revenue data is complicated, but still feasible, to obtain, and you will need it to establish the link between what salespeople and marketers do and the company's profits and losses. It will connect each of the indicators we've examined so far to bottom-line impact. Sometimes, you will be able to make that connection clearly and indisputably because cause and effect is straightforward, as in the case of redeeming a coupon or discount offer. Of course, this relationship is rarely so visible. In many situations, marketers will have to work with assumptions, statistics, and validation procedures in order to guarantee acceptability, reliability, and robustness of the data they collect.

To determine how many purchases the project has impacted, you can build a cause-effect relationship by using methods that include, but are not limited to:

- Control groups
- Regression analysis
- Questionnaires and surveys
- Corporations' own records
- Cluster analysis
- Conjoint analysis
- Trend line analysis
- Etc.

A few examples of how to use these methods:

> *Control groups:* A control group, also known as a mirror group, is a group of people that has not been exposed to the project under evaluation but that is otherwise under the same conditions for the same time period as the group impacted by the project. A control group evaluation is composed of two groups: the experimental group (the one that is exposed to the marketing or sales project, where changes are observed and

recorded) and the control group (the one that is not exposed to the project). If a change can be attributed directly and unequivocally to a project, there is no need to establish a control group. For the validity of conclusions drawn from the results of controlled projects, it is essential that the target groups assigned to the project be representative of the same population and be exposed to the same conditions. For instance, it would not be useful to implement a marketing project in the United States and compare its results to the German market, which was not exposed to the same marketing project. The reality, conditions, and even populations of these markets are completely different, and whatever change is recorded could not be directly linked to the project with an acceptable degree of certainty.

Trend line analysis: A trend is nothing more than the general direction in which a variable is headed. A *trend line* is formed when a straight line can be drawn between two or more equivalent points on a two-axis graphic. It starts from when the actual movement begins to be measured, and the more points it involves, the more reliable the trend. In sales and marketing, the usual equivalent points are the average or median values of the variable at stake (usually sales or business variables that can be converted to money). The critical point from the ROI Marketing point of view is the difference between the existing trend prior to the marketing project's execution and the way it evolves during and after the project has been executed. For this difference to be relevant, all variables must remain the same before project execution, during execution, and for as long as you continue to measure. If there is any change (for instance, the overall market grows), the results should be adjusted to account for the verified change. For instance, if the trend line shows that there is a sales increase of 10% and you know that the overall market grew by 3%, the actual growth that can be attributed to the project is 7% (10% growth minus 3% market growth = 7% growth attributable to the project, if all other variables remained the same).

Chart 3: Trend Line Analysis

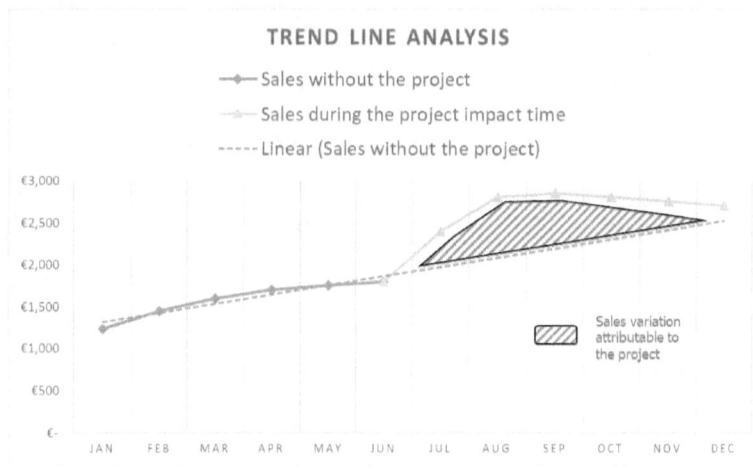

In some cases, companies already have relevant information that can be used to relate communication inputs to revenue. It is well known that the pharmaceutical industry has several tools to measure the impact of its marketing and sales efforts. Insurance companies also have sophisticated ways of recording the revenue generated through sales and marketing expenditures. Variables like customer lifetime value, conversion ratios, and attrition rates are only a few examples of these types of data. Furthermore, if a given company practices ROI Marketing, each measurement and evaluation serves as the basis for future measurement and evaluations.

Panel groups: Panel groups (rather than focus groups, which are qualitative-results driven) are a great way to infer statistically relevant information required to relate marketing or sales inputs to revenue. Panels are made of large samples of a population that respond to a set of questions. A large number of responses is collected in a statistically representative and relevant way, and margins of error and confidence levels are well known. There are some great customer-experience platforms that can gather the data needed to establish a cause-effect relationship.

Surveys and questionnaires: Surveys and questionnaires are an easy and very competitive way to collect statistically significant and indisputable data, and they can establish a cause-effect relationship between what happens at the marketing level and what happens at the business profit-and-loss level. But marketers have to be very careful and thoughtful when generating the questions they use.

The more direct and verified the correlations between marketing or sales inputs and revenue outputs, the more reliable and accepted your results will be. For instance, if it's possible to directly measure the entire target population (in the case of a niche market, such as business-to-business), there will be no questions regarding the data's accuracy and significance. As the direct link fades through population size, the relevance of data starts to weaken. If no direct measure of the full population is available, then a sample group could give an accurate and acceptable level of reliability. It is always good practice to validate such acceptability prior to using the criterion as a relating factor. When no direct measurement is possible (either of the full population or through a relevant sample population), then industry standards, historical records, and/or benchmarks can provide a valid correlation between project inputs from sales and marketing activities and revenue. Last, if no standards, records, or benchmarks are available (either internally or externally), key stakeholders' assumptions (corrected for confidence level) can also be considered.

Key stakeholders are all of those who deal with or are affected by the variable under measurement. They could be the company's own sales force, distribution channels, point-of-sale information (sellout, for instance), industry associations, consumers, directors, etc.

The following graphic shows some of the methods of converting project inputs into business results, along with their degree of indisputability. It is obvious that the stronger the link between the cause of the input and its effect on the business, the more indisputable the data will be.

Chart 4: Relating Effects & Indisputability of Data

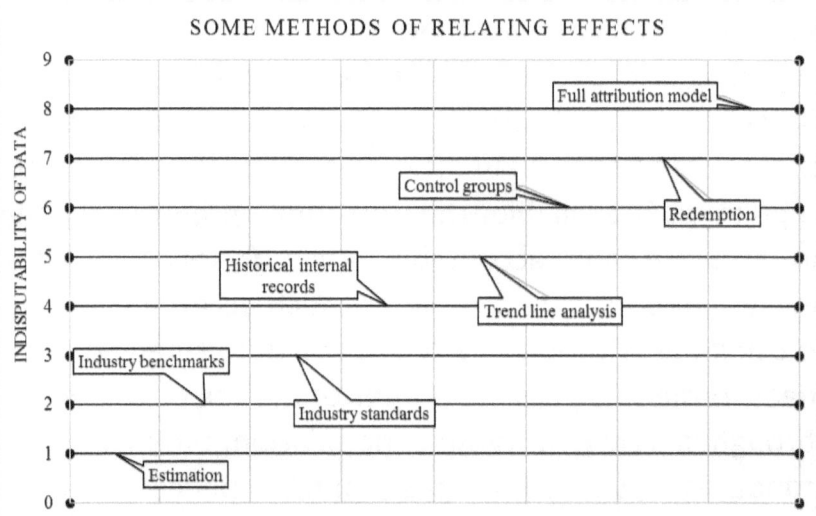

To answer the second question on page 126 – What was the influence of my project on each purchasing act? – it is necessary to define a decision-making pie for the target market of the given product or service.

It is well known that purchase decisions are made based on, and influenced by, a series of factors that range from the emotional to the rational insights of each customer or consumer.

Some of those factors are:

- Price
- Brand image/reputation
- Ease of purchase
- Post-sale service
- Warranty
- Recommendations
- Product features (flavor, color, etc.)
- Customer experience
- Delivery time
- Distribution proximity/delivery service
- Etc.

Each of these factors has a relative weight in the decision-making process and comes into play during the product and/or brand consideration, evaluation, purchase, and loyalty loop of the value chain. At each phase of the value chain, there are several marketing and sales tools that help the customer or consumer to move one step closer into actual purchase, purchase repetition, or recommendation.

One of the first tasks in determining the impact of a particular project on a purchasing decision is to define your customers' decision-making pie. Which factors are relevant to their purchase decision-making process? This pie should not be defined internally to avoid biased conclusions, but by asking your same clients in a statistically relevant and robust way, thereby combining self-explained and conjoint analysis.

Through this self-explained method and/or a discrete choice conjoint analysis, it will be possible to define the importance of each factor in each purchase decision – and, therefore, each factor's influence on the decision.

Another approach to determining the pie of purchasing-decision influences was introduced in 1987 by Jordan Louviere. This choice-based approach was initially called a Max-Diff study, then it evolved into best-worst scaling (BWS) and/or discrete choice experiment (DCE). Rather than using scales of importance or relative weight of features, this approach incorporated a new technique based on the much easier (for consumers) practice of choosing among pre-selected sets of options.

Whichever method you use, make sure you implement it rigorously and that it is mathematically validated.

Once the degree of influence is determined, that influence rate shall be applied to whichever margin we are considering as impacted by our marketing or sales project (product of the first isolation or relating factor). This process defines the actual revenue (income) generated by the project in a robust and credible way.

The margin or profit ratio we chose as the base for the actual return calculation emerges from the monetary conversion criteria to which we refer next.

- **Monetary Conversion Plan**

The Monetary Conversion Plan establishes the profitability baseline that will be used to determine the actual economic return (isolated by the relating factors) of the project under evaluation. Since we cannot consider sales as the final result of our marketing or sales project (we can increase sales at a loss), we must define the return or net revenue: the actual profit (or loss) generated by the project. The baseline from which to do this is the value that will be set as the profit for each individual unit under consideration. If you are selling cars, for example, it should be the profit for each car sold. If you are selling insurance, it could be the value of each client or of each policy in the impacted segment. If you are selling medical equipment, it could be the profit generated by the sales of each piece of equipment, plus the profit generated by subsequent services (if that extra value is defined and netted from all other expenses).

Through the Monetary Conversion Plan and the use of relating factors, we link sales and marketing inputs (marketing performance) to business outputs (economic results or profit).

It is important to understand what I mean when I use the words "revenue" and "return." For the ROI

Marketing Matrix, "revenue" represents the inflow of money as a result of sales and marketing activities (attributable revenues). It refers to the revenue generated mainly through sales, although it may be originated from other sources such as donations. "Return" or "gross return" refers to revenues minus costs of goods sold and fixed indirect costs. "Net return" (the actual return on marketing investment) refers to the return attributed to a marketing project, minus money invested into the project (direct costs) and fixed costs that behave as direct costs to the project, such as the time spent by marketing department staff on the activity.

This last result, net return, will be the ROI of our marketing projects or campaigns.

Chart 5: Revenue vs. Return

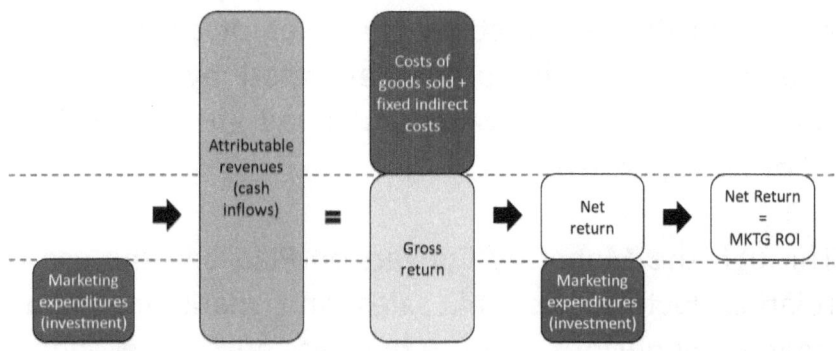

CASE IV: ROI Marketing Cascade – About Monetary Conversion

Industry: Dairy Products
Type of organization: National; Country leader (Mexico)
Offering: B2C

Introduction:
Fast-moving consumer goods (FMCG) are always a battleground where large multinational and local players fight for market share and shelf space with low margins and large volumes. The marketing battlefield (marketing mix) is mainly conventional advertising, digital marketing, point-of-sale activities, and sponsorships.

The company's goal:
This case is about a big player that wanted to determine the actual return of a sponsorship program. The program took place during a period of three months and was advertised on TV, on digital media, and at the point of sale. The promotion consisted of a series of collectible packaging SKUs (stock keeping units) branded with the colors and emblem of each participating team in the sports league. By buying one of the sponsored products, consumers earned the right to participate in several weekly sweepstakes for televisions and tickets to the major final of the sport. Consumers were expected to collect the different packages and participate in the incentive sweepstakes, thereby increasing sales and generating a positive return. The promotion ran on six

different product categories. The challenge was to assign a monetary value to each purchase influenced by the promotion and to determine the ROI of the sponsorship program.

How did they achieve it?
The marketing team began by defining the relating factors that isolated the number of purchases impacted by the campaign and the influence the sponsorship project had on each purchase. The marketing team then realized they had to overcome an internal challenge: The company had prohibited the disclosure of actual product margins to anybody outside the finance and accounting department. The lack of a reference figure for each type of product could prevent them from determining the actual ROI of the sponsorship program for each product line. It also revealed a serious internal communication problem: How could the marketing department be accountable for its strategy without the ability to know the actual impact of its activities on the bottom line of the business?

What was the result?
This challenge did not dampen the intention of the marketing team to be accountable in a visible and credible way. They decided to use, as a monetary conversion criterion, the overall EBITDA (earnings before interest, taxes, depreciation, and amortization) of the business. It was agreed that once the model was run, a dashboard would be delivered to the finance and accounting department for it to plug in the actual

product margins and determine the return for each of the six categories. But a relevant question emerged again: What would the finance and accounting department do with the results (whatever they might be)? If it kept them for itself, the marketing department could not use them to improve. If it shared the results with the marketing department, then the non-disclosure rule would be broken.

First, all marketing costs (not just for this project) had to be subtracted from the EBITDA figure in order to identify the actual margin without marketing expenditures. Without doing this, the department could not have subtracted the actual sponsorship investment from the attributed profits. Sure, making calculations without discounting the marketing expenditures would have given a return figure. However, it would have not been as accurate as one that subtracted the actual investment, as it would include other business operational efficiencies or inefficiencies, showing the average profitability of all product categories (including those that were not in promotion) and all channels (including distribution channels that did not run the promotion).

The EBITDA of the business was recalculated without the overall marketing budget, and it turned out to be 12% (our profitability baseline). With this EBITDA, the return on the sponsorship program was negative.

This experience helped the company recognize the limitations imposed by the non-disclosure rule. It led management to overturn the rule, and the marketing team learned the actual margin for each product category. Those margins were higher than 12% in all cases (more than double in some cases), showing the importance of the marketing department's strategic decisions about product mixes for promotions. In the studied sponsorship promotion, the campaign was profitable for only one product category, and lost money for the others, making the overall return on investment negative.

Conclusions:
Never give up on your quest to calculate the actual economic return of sales and marketing campaigns. Although you will most likely encounter a series of difficulties, you will be able to overcome them with patience, determination, rigor, and relevance. Sometimes, you have to walk the wrong way to show it is wrong. Wise management will never give up on profitability improvement – their bonuses depend on it.

4. ROI Marketing Cascade: ROI Sensitivity Analysis

The ROI Sensitivity Analysis is the fourth stage of the ROI Marketing Cascade.

As a reminder, the ROI Marketing Cascade is the planning phase of ROI Marketing, in which you determine, prior to investing, whether the project could make or lose money if objectives are met. It is also the phase during which you match the allocated budget to the impact needed to achieve those goals, as well as the project break-even point.

The ROI Sensitivity Analysis entails generating predictive models based on changing variables under your control and showing how those changes would affect the actual economic output of the project. These two processes, validation and prediction, represent two of the four functionalities of the ROI Marketing Matrix. I will discuss validation and prediction in Part 3, which covers the functionalities and uses of monitoring the economic impact of sales and marketing projects.

CASE V: ROI Marketing Cascade – About ROI Sensitivity Analysis (Validation)

Industry: Toiletries
Type of organization: Multinational company (Germany)
Offering: B2C

Introduction:
Household and toiletries is a very complicated sector. Highly dependent on volatile oil prices, this industry almost constantly sees its margins grow and shrink, with very little room for price changes at the consumer level. It is highly commoditized, and business players depend on heavy marketing to differentiate their products.

The company's goal:
This client company intended to gain shelf space and market share by doing a point-of-sale campaign that offered an incentive (a giveaway) in exchange for the purchase of two units of the same product. They wanted to make sure they had a chance for a positive return on the campaign, even with volatile pricing changes in their main raw material.

How did they achieve it?
A full validation of objectives and break-even point was calculated for the whole campaign. The sales department reviewed and checked the results for financial viability. The campaign was supposed to cover 1,000 points of sale at large distribution chains. Material

explaining the campaign would be the only support at the point of sale. It would be paired with specific information on the web and pushed through digital media. The point-of-sale and web/digital information were supposed to drive sales. The overall campaign investment (including point-of-sale material, distribution, creative fees, incentives, etc.) was €99,600. Each product sold for €2.00 per unit. The plan was for each point of sale to have one display that contained 34 units of product to be sold each month. The margin per product sold would be 30%. The objective was to sell 100% of the product in promotion during the two months the campaign would last.

What was the result?
A quick verification revealed that, even if the company achieved the objective of selling 100% of the product on promotional shelves, the campaign would lose money.

Investment: € 99,600
Revenue from sales: €136,000 (68,000 units sold)
Margin: € 40,800 (30%)
Return (value):   -€58,800
Return (ROI):   -59%

Furthermore, the break-even point of the project showed that sales would have to increase by 144% just for the campaign to pay for itself. Needless to say, the sales department considered this unachievable, and the campaign was redesigned with a more affordable budget of €13,450. With this lower investment, the company sold only 40% of the product on promotion – but had a positive ROI of 21%.

Conclusions:
Validating the objectives and finding a commercial break-even point is key to minimizing marketing-project risks. In this case, it saved the company thousands of euros and allowed it to rethink and redesign the campaign. The redesigned campaign served the same purpose, but withstood the validation and prediction scenarios in the ROI Sensitivity Analysis. (Note that in this case, the isolation measured accounted for 100% of sales, which is not correct.)

Summary bullets:

- No project should start without knowing the organization pillars. Those pillars are the mission and vision, as well as general sales and marketing plans. Pillars are the foundation of objectives.

- Objectives should always have measurable indicators, a time frame (period of influence of the project), and clear quantitative thresholds for each type of objective. Always check for alignment with the pillars.

- No evaluation can be done without proper planning. Make sure you plan for relating factors (attribution model), monetization criteria, and data collection.

- Conduct an ROI Sensitivity Analysis, as this will help with the go-no-go decision-making process, validating the project prior to investment and establishing predictive models that will provide solid criteria to check the project's potential.

ROI Marketing Matrix Phase 2: The ROI Marketing Ladder

Once the ROI Marketing Cascade is finished and the "go" decision has been made, the project or campaign enters the execution phase, known as the ROI Marketing Ladder. This includes both the execution of the project as planned and the execution of the steps to conclude the evaluation cycle.

In this book, I will not talk about the execution of the project itself, as this is unique for each project and varies greatly. I will mention the steps needed to extract the greatest possible value out of measuring the actual economic return of the project under evaluation.

There are four stages to measuring the ROI of ongoing marketing or sales projects (during the execution phase):

1. ROI Marketing Ladder: Data Collection

Once you have decided to go ahead with your project and have planned your work – the Data Collection Plan of the ROI Marketing Cascade phase – it's time to work your plan. Data collection includes not only gathering information related to the indicators (marketing performance, cost, and revenue), but also organizing the logistics and infrastructure for storing and managing the information. It entails things like tabulation, the capability to extract data and to run diverse and multiple queries, compatibility with data visualization software, etc. At this stage, a business data analyst should address and secure the above-mentioned needs, and ensure data is treated properly in order to run analyses and obtain valid conclusions. Statistical relevance, data robustness, and proper and accurate information management systems require that IT, sales, and marketing work together.

Planning for evaluation and validating projects for their expected economic return should bring the sales and marketing departments together (if they were not already merged). Validating a project entails checking its commercial viability, and that cannot be done by the marketing department alone. Nor can maximizing sales from the execution of any marketing project. Working together is a must in order to indisputably connect marketing and sales efforts to the business.

Additionally, IT must play a role in providing business intelligence services throughout the ROI Marketing Cascade. The constant evolution of technology and the ever-growing reach of "digital behaviors" has helped evolve data collection in ways not even imagined only 10 years ago.

2. ROI Marketing Ladder: Relating
Correlation does not mean causation, so in order to derive causation from an observation, you must be able to relate marketing inputs (positioning, education, and interactions) to business outputs (costs, revenues, and return). This is why the relating factors are defined during the ROI Marketing Cascade phase. During the ROI

Marketing Ladder phase – the execution phase – you must define which actual purchases were impacted by the project under evaluation and how much your project influenced those specific purchase decisions, based on the pre-defined relating factors. The output of relating is a number of interactions and a rate of influence. The result of this process is key to building robustness around the whole evaluation, and it is the foundation of credibility. These two factors, once isolated, will be the base to attribute value during the monetary conversion step coming up next. In short, you will end up with a number of impacts and a rate of influence.

This is achieved through the isolation methods selected in the Data Collection Plan, such as control groups, trend line analysis, conjoint analysis, etc.

The relating process implies that each performance indicator should be accounted for at whichever dimension you measure (and you should try to measure in at least five dimensions of measurement). Take the example of a car manufacturer that is planning to launch a new feature for a model that is already in the market. The plan is to conduct a branding campaign at multi-brand dealers, where the company wants consumers to associate this new feature (called "PGT") with its brand and experience its benefits on test drives. The company hopes this will increase sales. The table that follows shows how each indicator is accounted for at each dimension of measurement.

Table 5: Relating New-Car Feature Campaign: Performance Indicators in Each Measurement Dimension

Type of Indicator	Example of Indicator to Be Collected	1st Question for Monetary Conversion = # of Impacts	2nd Question = Degree of Influence
Positioning	Brand awareness level	How many consumers have seen the brand because of the project?	What is the influence of the brand on customers' purchase decision?
Education	Knowledge about the new feature	How many people learned about the new feature?	What is the influence of the feature on the purchase decision?
Interaction	Test drives	How many people took the test drive?	What is the influence of the test drive on the purchase decision?
Cost	Cost per test drive + educational tools + branding	What is the cost of a test drive and of other educational and branding tools?	What was the overall investment for this project?
Revenue	Car price	What is the actual sales price collected in each sale?	What was the overall income generated by this project?

Remember that in order to determine the degree of influence of positioning, education, and interaction factors, you must define the decision-making pie for these specific types of transactions. This is done as part of the Relating Factors Plan and Data Collection Plan during the ROI Marketing Cascade (planning phase). Without knowing this degree of influence, you will be isolating the purchases impacted by your project, attributing 100% of the profits to your project – which you know is not accurate. Failing to attribute the correct portion of profits to your project will hinder the credibility of the whole process and will most likely make your results questionable (if not entirely unreliable).

3. ROI Marketing Ladder: Converting

The next step is to convert the number of purchases impacted and percentage of influence on each purchase into monetary values. There will be two main outputs: costs and revenues (gross income). In this phase, you must try to convert the indicators measured during data collection into money, to the extent possible.

Going back to the example of the car manufacturer, the project included collecting information in six different dimensions of measurement: positioning, education, interactions, costs, revenues, and return. The following table shows the data collected during the execution of the project. (The numbers included are just examples; in real life, they will always be the results of your Data Collection Plan):

Table 6: Indicators Monetization Reference Sheet

Type of Indicator	Example of Indicator	Impact	Degree of Influence
Positioning	Brand awareness level	1,200 people	3%
Education	Knowledge about the new car feature	860 people	8%
Interaction	Test drives	3,500 interactions	30%
Cost	Cost per test drive + educational tools + branding	Test drive = $40 Point of sale (educational tools + branding) = $50,000	$190,000
Revenue	Car price tag	$32,000 x 1,200 cars sold to people impacted by the campaign	$38,400,000

The following table breaks down how many purchases were actually affected by the project's different tools (branding at the point of sale, knowledge of a new feature, and test drives):

	Brand	Feature	Test Drive
Brand only	260		
Feature only		0	
Test drive only			0
Brand & feature only	800	800	
Brand & test drive only	90		90
Test drive & feature		10	10
All three tools	50	50	50
	1,200	860	150

4. ROI Marketing Ladder: ROI Analysis

Having obtained costs and revenues, the mathematical calculations are straightforward. However, this is not the end of the ROI Marketing Ladder. A thorough analysis will generate much more value than just knowing whether a project was profitable or not. Conclusions, recommendations, and a full set of business intelligence data are the main outputs of this final step in the evaluation cycle of a project or campaign.

Continuing with the car manufacturer example:
Costs: $190,000
Revenues: $38,400,000

The overall influence of the project on the decision-making process is 41% – the total of the degree of influence of branding, point-of-sale material, and test drives from Table 6. This means that the decision to buy a car is also influenced by other factors, such as price, good service, financing, word-of-mouth, etc., that account for 59% of the purchasing decision. There are several profitability scenarios, depending on the impact and degree of influence of those diverse tools in the decision-making process.

Assuming each car delivers a gross margin (without including marketing expenses) of $2,800, the total profit from car sales impacted by one or a combination of the three tools was $3,360,000 (1,200 car sales impacted X gross margin). By now, you know you cannot attribute 100% of that margin to the project, since there are factors outside the project (part of the customer decision-making pie) that influenced those purchases. Hence, the overall direct return attributable to the project is:

Impact x Degree of Influence x Gross Margin

	Impact	% influence	Actual net margin attributed
Brand Awareness	1,200 people bought the car and saw the ad with the brand	3%	$100,800
Feature Knowledge	860 people who bought the car learned about the new feature beforehand	8%	$192,640
Test Drive	150 people who purchased did the test drive	30%	$126,000
Total			$419,440

If the cost of the marketing project (now treated as an investment) was $190,000, we now know that the economic return on this project was positive, and the actual ROI was:

$$\frac{\text{Return - Investment}}{\text{Investment}}$$

or

$$\frac{\$419{,}440 - \$190{,}000}{\$190{,}000} = 1.21$$

ROI of the project: 121%

But this is by no means the only information to extract from this analysis. The ROI evaluation allows managers to generate business intelligence that should be used for future planning. What was the actual return for each tool? Can we separate them? What would happen if we didn't have the point-of-sale material? Would we have achieved the same results? What about without test drives? This is the moment when thorough analysis can deliver highly valuable information for future planning (beyond just project evaluation).

Some of the valuable business intelligence that can be extracted from this evaluation of the car manufacturer marketing program includes:

1. Conversion ratios

What conversion ratios can we extract from this evaluation that will help to plan for desired results in the future?

Branding reach: 100,000 target people
Education reach: 18,000 people
Test drive reach: 3,500 test drives
Sales (in units):   1,200 cars

Hence, most people would calculate the following ratios:

Cars sold per brand impressions: 1 car/83 impressions (100,000 impressions/1,200 cars sold)

Cars sold per education reach (POS material): 1 car/15 impacts (18,000 impacts/1,200 cars sold)

Cars sold per test drives: 1 car/3 test drives (3,500 test drives/1,200 cars sold)

But this is wrong, since you can talk about a brand impression alone (people who saw the POS material without paying attention to the new feature being presented), but you cannot consider the education message alone – since all people who saw the education message also saw the branding impact. In addition, you should consider those sales that were really impacted by each tool. In this case, you should calculate the following ratios:

Cars sold per brand impressions: 1 car/83 impressions (100,000 impressions/1,200 cars sales impacted)

Cars sold per education reach (POS material): 1 car/21 impacts (18,000 impacts/860 cars sales impacted)

Cars sold per test drives: 1 car/23 test drives (3,500 test drives/150 cars sales impacted)

These figures reflect the real conversion from each tool. So, next time the sales and marketing director sees that the business plan for the coming year includes the challenge of growing overall annual sales by 10% (let's say this means selling 10,000 more cars), he or she knows which tools to use to get there. In this case, it could be done by investing in a combination of POS material and test drives, which will most likely need to impact 1,250,000 branding impressions, 209,302 education impacts, and 233,333 test drives.

As you can see, given the scale of having to do 233,333 test drives or almost 210,000 education impacts, it would probably not be feasible to sell 10,000 more cars through these tools. Thanks to the business intelligence gained through previous evaluations, it is possible to know the objective cannot be achieved with tools that, even if they were successful for one set of goals, may not be viable for this year's business plan, given real traffic to the dealers.

2. Profitability of tools

Using the business intelligence gained from this evaluation, it is also possible to isolate each type of tool to see how profitable they are independently. In this case, we will split them between point-of-sale material (branded displays showing the new feature, therefore combining both branding and new-feature education) with an overall investment of $50,000, and test drives with an overall investment of $140,000.

Tool	Investment	Revenue	Return	ROI
POS	$50,000	$293,440	$243,440	487%
Test drive	$140,000	$126,000	-$14,000	-10%
Total	$190,000	$419,440	$229,440	121%

It's important to review these results in depth to avoid jumping to incorrect conclusions. One such incorrect conclusion could be to assume that, because test drives alone are not profitable, they should be stopped. Similarly, it would be incorrect to conclude that, because POS material profitability is high, the entire budget should be invested into this material. Because the influence of a test drive is rather large in customers' decision-making pie (30% of the buy-no-buy decision), you might expect the conversion ratio for this tool to be higher than it actually is in this example. Twenty-three test drives to sell one car is even worse than the conversion ratio of an education impact (one car sold for every 21 education impacts). That suggests that, in this case, education about a new feature is more effective than test driving the car. However, we know this is wrong since the test drive had a 30% influence on the buying decision, yet knowing about a new feature had only an 8% influence. This data can lead one to think that either education has been executed outrageously well or test drives were not executed correctly and efficiently (3,500 test drives over only 150 sales influenced buyers, hence its negative ROI). This is an activity to revise and analyze in terms of its real effectiveness and implementation performance.

3. Relative impact on business

The $229,440 net profit from this sales and marketing project represents 6.83% of the overall gross margin generated by the sales of those 1,200 cars. That is close to the overall business margin in this case (8.75% =

$2,800/$32,000 car price). In theory, you should not expect marketing and sales projects individually to be more profitable than the business itself. Your sales and marketing projects contribute to the overall profitability of the business, but they are not "your business."

In this case, this indicator tells you that, the next time you are planning, you will be able to set a profitability objective (the sixth dimension of measurement in the ROI Marketing Matrix). It also makes a strong argument against undesirable wishful thinking about return objectives that are subjectively set and distanced from reality.

In addition, this indicator defines the actual opportunity cost of not doing this project, or what the expected return should be when considering alternative projects.

This is not an exhaustive list of the valuable information you can extract from an ROI evaluation cycle. The conversion ratios, profitability of tools, and relative impact on business are key for future planning, but they do not represent, by any means, all the business intelligence you can extract from an evaluation. Although these results could be far from reality (remember, this is just an example), they serve to show some relevant conclusions, define and evaluate the individual performance of tools of a marketing mix, identify and revise possible flaws during execution, improve future planning and minimize risks, avoid known loses, increase known profits, and contribute to the overall organization and its pillars.

Summary bullets:

- Set up your objectives thoroughly in all six dimensions of measurement: positioning, education messages, interactions, costs, revenues, and returns.

- Focus on delivery rather than on execution.

- Establish a cause-effect relationship between marketing and its economic impact on the business.

- Plan your data collection. Use the 3WH checklist.

- Assign a monetary value to marketing performance indicators.

- Validate all your criteria prior to using them as part of the ROI Marketing management model.

- Keep track of all your investments (marketing expenditures, until you prove a net return) and affected costs (those impacted by the project).

- Plan your work and work your plan.

- Generate and use business intelligence to plan future projects and campaigns.

Part 3: Marketing & Sales Economics – What Is It Good For?

Chapter IV:
The Four Functionalities of an ROI Marketing Management Model

Introduction

Most companies do not evaluate the economic return of sales and marketing projects, and this is a dangerous practice. Those organizations never know whether the sales and marketing tactics they implement are profitable. They infer that, if the overall business is profitable, what they are doing must be right. But nothing could be further from the truth. Many CEOs and general managers tend to identify the operational inefficiencies in any organization. However, they seldom know where those inefficiencies are in marketing. In this discipline, intuition ends up playing a big role, and marketing budgets become an adjustable variable of the overall business's cash flow statements and profit and loss accounts.

Additionally, if you ask whether it is important to measure the economic return of a sales or marketing project, most managers will tell you that it is. But if you ask whether doing so is urgent, you will most likely encounter nodding heads or shrugged shoulders.

More and more, companies are recognizing how important it is to measure the actual economic return of marketing investments. However, since it is often not considered urgent, most organizations delay the decision to do so. Sadly, by the time marketers and/or managers realize they're facing an eventual negative impact from such an investment, it is already too late to take action. "It is not urgent" has become measurement's epitaph. Furthermore, if bosses, clients, or stakeholders identify or become aware of this loss, it impacts marketing and sales professionals directly, casting the individuals in a negative light.

It is clear and intuitive that measuring the return of any investment will indicate the actual profit generated by the investment. In addition, the perspective of planning, executing, and monitoring a marketing or sales project with an eye towards its economic impact opens a whole new world of possibilities. It will not only show the profits generated by the project, but it will also help managers make wiser decisions – thereby minimizing risks and maximizing profits for the overall organization.

How does ROI Marketing do this?

ROI Marketing is a way of managing sales and marketing plans, in general, and budgets, in particular. It is a management model. This way of working leads organizations into managing marketing and sales initiatives with a focus on results, rather than on execution. It also generates a cross-functional performance indicator that can be integrated into any type of sales and marketing project individually, or aggregated for a campaign or annual plan.

The ROI Marketing management model facilitates uses beyond the mere act of measuring a given return and evaluating the actual economic return of a project. As we saw when talking about ROI Analysis in the previous chapter, there are several observations, findings, and conclusions that can be extracted from the data collected during the period of influence of the project. Certain performance indicators, ratios, and results that appear as the conclusions of an evaluation cycle become the input for future project planning, incorporating business intelligence that will build in additional robustness to sales and marketing planning, thereby minimizing risks and increasing the chances of economic profitability. The way to do this is by evolving through different stages during the lifecycle of a project and/or campaign. These stages happen before, during, and after the project is executed.

The first two stages occur during the planning phase and prior to the project kickoff. During this period, managers need information that helps them decide whether or not to go ahead with the project. What type of information would be helpful and useful to the decision-making manager? If we are talking about ROI Marketing as a management model, we should look for ways to determine in advance whether our project will make money or not, if we are successful. This first functionality is called "Validation." Validation, however, is not the only pre-kickoff functionality of the ROI Marketing management model. For decision-makers, it can be useful to model plausible scenarios to check the sensitivity of the project to various factors that are under the company's control. This functionality is called "Prediction."

Once the decision to go with the project is made, it will become necessary to evaluate the project's real economic impact. This is one of the main objectives of this management model: to determine the actual return that each marketing or sales project or campaign generates. This functionality is called "Evaluation." And last, but far from least, the ROI Marketing management model offers an opportunity to extract information that serves as business intelligence for future projects and business planning. Since this directly affects the way managers plan for the future, this functionality is called "Planning."

Summarizing, the ROI Marketing management model generates value through four functionalities (in sequence):

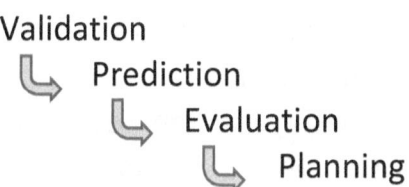

- *Functionality 1: Validation*

The scenario for validation is that of achieving the project objectives. After all, that's what we set objectives for, to reach them. So, if the project achieves its objectives, will the company make money? The validation process works with the known costs of the project and the monetary conversion criteria. It uses the criteria to assign financial values to the sales and marketing inputs generated by reaching 100% of the objectives, and it transforms those inputs into revenues. Once the costs and revenues generated by the project are known, you can calculate the ROI of the project if it achieves its goals. This process, which seems so simple and obvious, is almost never completed.

Validation also entails finding the commercial break-even point of the project. What does this mean? It basically responds to the question: What influence does this project need to exert on sales for it to pay for itself? This is the point at which costs are covered, but it does not speak to whether the project was ultimately profitable. Put another way: Where is the break-even point of the project in terms of needed sales? This is a crucial point and a moment of revelation within ROI Marketing as a management tool. It means that marketing and sales should get together and review the project from both perspectives: implementing marketing activities and the commercial potential of such activities to impact sales. It brings sales and marketing together (as they should always be), with common tools and a shared performance indicator. If, for instance, a project needs to lead to a 30% increase in annual sales to pay for itself in two months, it will most likely not be viable from the economic return point of view (of course, this is an extreme example, but it serves to portray the picture).

Validation also serves to check your objectives. Sometimes, managers, pressed by the need for business results and demands from higher levels of the company, tend to use overly optimistic objectives. Unrealistic objectives, or "guesstimates" of results a project should achieve, are dangerous propositions. When objectives are not realistic, they lack credibility and, even if they are measurable, they represent a leap to nowhere. Not knowing where you are going, you may wind up anywhere. In business, this is not an option.

The validation process starts by assuming that the project will achieve the results stipulated in its objectives. Again, these results should cover at least five dimensions of measurement: positioning, education, interactions, costs, and revenues.

In our previous case of the car manufacturer and its POS/test drive program, let's assume that the company initially had the following objectives:

Positioning objective:
"To see our brand name and image (branding) as innovative, by having at least 100,000 impressions of our new creativity at our dealer network (points of sale) during the three-month campaign."

Education objective:
"To associate our brand name and image (branding) as the only brand with PGT (new feature), by having at

least 75% of car sales impacted by knowledge of the new feature at our dealer network (points of sale) during the three-month campaign."

Interactions objective:
"To support the communications campaign with experiential marketing, by having at least 2,000 drivers test our models with PGT during the three months of the campaign."

Cost objective:
"To spend, during the three-month campaign, no more than the $150,000 we spent on last year's POS campaign."

Revenue objective:
"To influence at least 1,000 car sales during the three months of the campaign."

Now let's run the scenario of achieving these objectives.

In the case of validation, since we have not implemented the project yet, we need to assume that it will meet all objectives. So, in this case, we actually influenced 1,000 car sales with the three tools.

Since the validation functionality is done after planning for data collection, relating factors, and monetary conversion criteria, in this case, we already know the influence of our project on consumers' decision-making process: branding had a 3% influence on each purchase decision, the new feature 8%, and test drives 30%. We also know the monetary conversion criteria: $2,800 profit per car sold. (This is based on work begun in Chapter III – The ROI Marketing Ladder.)

In the case of positioning, we assume that we reached the 100,000 impressions mark and the 1,000 cars mark due to the influence of the branding campaign. For education, we will assume that the proportion stays as we set it in the objective, so only 75% of car purchases were influenced by the new-feature education campaign. In the case of the test drives, it would be fair to assume that only a portion of total sales will be impacted by them. If previous ratios are not available, it is necessary to assume the most conservative scenario. In this case, we chose to assume (based on past experience) that 10% of cars sold were really influenced by the test drive. Costs are assumed as per project budget planning – in this case, $40 per test drive and $50,000 total for POS communication. Finally, revenues come from car sales – in this case, 1,000 cars sold.

Under this scenario:

Tool	Objective	Influence of project	Generated profits
Brand	1,000 cars sold	3% of $2,800	$84,000
Feature	750 cars sold	8% of $2,800	$168,000
Test drive	100 cars	30% of $2,800	$84,000
			$336,000

Actual cost if objectives achieved:

Test drives	2,000	$40.00	$80,000
POS			$50,000
			$130,000

Under this scenario, profits would be $206,000, equivalent to 158% ROI, if all objectives are met.

Another validation scenario is the break-even point of the project. We must first define the breakeven in terms of goals to achieve (number of cars sold) and then validate this figure in terms of its relative impact on the overall sales of the period. This validation aligns the sales and marketing departments. And, it allows marketing to be visibly and accountably tied to business, and not only to communication.

In this case, continuing with the car manufacturer example, the company sells 100,000 cars per year, and each car sold has a gross profit (excluding marketing expenses) of $2,800. In the scenario where this project meets its objectives, the total marketing investment would be $130,000. And, if all three tools influence a purchase, the project will have influenced 41% of purchasers' decision-making processes. Therefore, only $1,148 of gross profit per car sale can be attributed to the three tools of the campaign. This means that the campaign must lead to 114 car sales in order to pay for itself. If, on average, the company sells 8,335 cars per month (in the real world, this figure would need to be adjusted by seasonality for the three months of the campaign) and the campaign lasts three months, the campaign break-even point represents just 0.4% of sales during its influence period. So, the question to validate with the salesforce is: Can the campaign influence 0.4% of sales in this three-month period? If the answer is yes, something positive and relevant has happened: Sales and marketing are aligned and believe in the execution of this project. It is not just a marketing project; it is a business project that implements sales and marketing tactics.

To summarize, during the validation process, managers generate two scenarios: economic results if objectives are achieved and commercial viability through a break-even point scenario.

The first validation functionality is completed, and we see that achieving the objectives is a profitable proposition to the business. Is this enough? Although we have a new non-biased criterion to support a go-no-go decision, most likely this is not completely exhaustive. A complete ROI Sensitivity Analysis could give us a hint of what may happen along the way. This analysis is carried by completing the second functionality of the ROI Marketing management model: prediction.

- *Functionality 2: Prediction*

Prediction works the same way as validation, but it generates diverse scenarios by changing the variables that are under the manager's control. In most sales and marketing projects, managers in charge can make a series of discretionary decisions that will impact the costs and the performance of the project. Those decisions are mostly related to the execution of the project, an execution that has not started in this stage but is already planned and ready to go. So, what happens if you change some of those variables under control?

In the car manufacturer example, several relevant factors are under the manager's control: number of dealers, cost per test drive, objectives, type and quantity of POS material, method of delivery, personnel devoted to the test drives, creative material, etc. Each of them will affect the economic outcome of the project and generate different plausible scenarios that will help to fine-tune implementation, with the aim of being both effective and profitable.

Going beyond our example scenario, what if the initiative is supported with more-expensive incentives? What if the time frame is extended? What about more television commercials? If a distribution center is changed? These questions might be asked of any other variable that a manager can change at will, within given limitations.

When Validation and Prediction Results Are Negative:
The three steps mentioned so far — two validation steps and one prediction step — occur prior to investment, so

they support the go-no-go decision-making process. What happens if the results of the validation and prediction are negative or don't look so good?

The validation and prediction steps, which make up the ROI Sensitivity Analysis, serve several purposes:

- Determine in advance whether the project will/could make or lose money if goals are met.
- Find the commercial break-even point of the project.
- Minimize risks.
- Allow you to take preventive actions in case results are negative or indicate a risk that the project will be a money-losing proposition.
- Increase ROI Marketing awareness and support within the organization.
- Improve the chances of a positive economic return on sales and marketing investments.

If the predicted results don't look very good or are too close to money-losing for comfort, you can take several actions.

Prediction Scenario 1:

If the project loses money

- Seek ways to reduce costs without compromising results.
- Review your objectives; maybe you should be more ambitious.
- Consider canceling the project or looking for alternatives that can deliver the same with less.
- Increase your knowledge; generate key learnings.

Remember, when a project loses money, the fact that the department or the organization doesn't know about it doesn't mean that the project stops generating losses. Sooner or later, the consequences of inaction will take a toll.

When projects are too close to the break-even point, it is dangerous to assume that they pose no economic risk. Being at the edge of profitability in a predictive model should be seen as predicting a loss, and all efforts should be made to increase the changes of profitability. Being conservative adds credibility to the overall analysis and makes your recommendations for action more robust and attention-worthy.

Prediction Scenario 2:

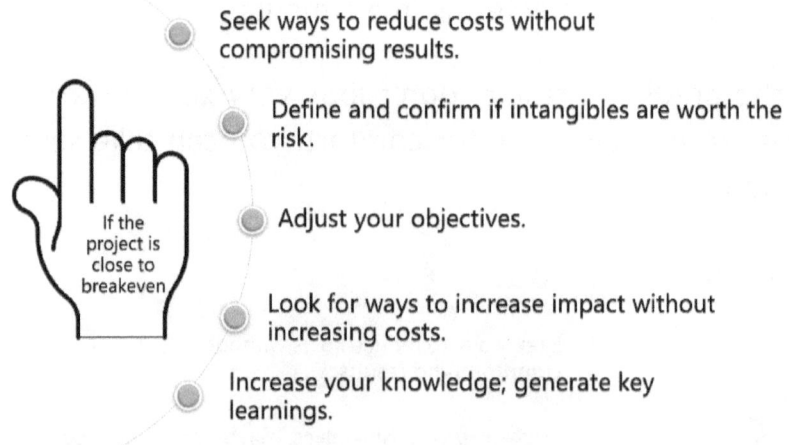

A predictive model does not guarantee success; it only offers more information that will help you to make more-educated decisions while minimizing risks.

Beware that the job of the manager in this prediction stage is not to portray optimistic outcomes, but rather, the most conservative and plausible scenarios based on inputs from the market (clients, sales force, market surveys, internal research, etc.) – including a "most likely" scenario based also on these inputs. This exercise will provide several outcomes, some of which might be positive.

So, what happens if the initial modelling predicts a positive and profitable picture?

Prediction Scenario 3:

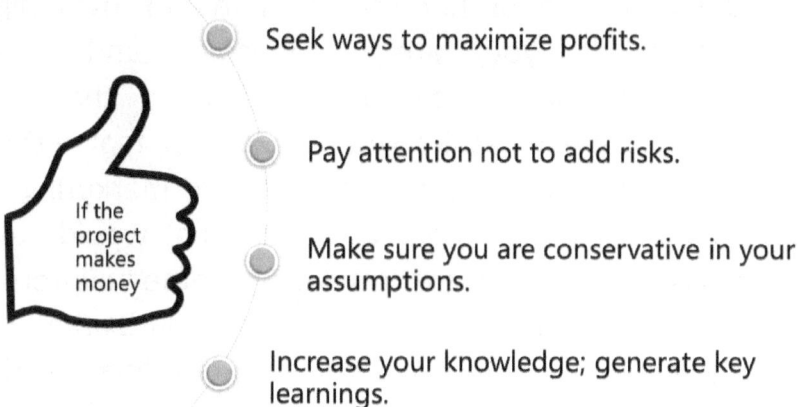

If the project makes money

- Seek ways to maximize profits.
- Pay attention not to add risks.
- Make sure you are conservative in your assumptions.
- Increase your knowledge; generate key learnings.

But the whole story of sales and marketing accountability does not only affect your project, it can also affect your position and even your career! Of course, all these types of decisions will have an impact not only on the business, but also on your position. You may worry: What if the project (which you've been working on for the last five years, by the way) loses money? Will it be canceled? Will you suffer any negative impact?

It is very hard to know if the projects you did in the past performed in the same way as the one you are evaluating now. It is quite hazardous to assume that if this year's project lost money, all past ones lost money as well. But this applies also if a project is profitable. Unless you repeat cycles of evaluation, it is not possible to extract conclusions about past performance.

Fearing a negative impact from a negative ROI evaluation is the equivalent of a doctor fearing a patient would blame him or her for the patient's own high cholesterol. If you are responsible and have recommended and/or executed a project that had negative economic results, you should not fear either. You've just discovered a way to improve marketing or sales planning and stop a profit bleed that would have otherwise gone unnoticed. You have become an internal consultant improving processes and procedures that will have a positive impact on the bottom line of the organization. By running an evaluation and facing negative results, you are showing your professional skills, analytical competence, ability to think and look outside the box, and business alignment capabilities. Hence, a marketer or sales manager should never be afraid of whatever result an evaluation cycle will bring. After all, when analyzing a project or campaign, you are not evaluating the professional performance of a person, but rather, the project and/or campaign's potential or actual economic contribution to the business.

However, delivering negative results should never be like shooting yourself in the foot. If results are negative, it is always advisable to report the results together with key learnings that will help the company avoid the same negative consequences in the future. It is also advisable to offer recommendations for alternatives to achieve the desired results with a positive economic return in the future.

Case VI: ROI Marketing Management – About ROI Sensitivity Analysis (Validation and Prediction – Predictive Modelling)

Industry: Food
Type of organization: Multinational company (France)
Offering: B2C

Introduction:
Frozen food products have some logistics limitations due to the need to maintain and have traceability of the cold chain they must observe. In most cases, manufacturers must rely on local distributors with cold storage capabilities that can serve demand from points of sale in a timely fashion. In the case of this client, the distribution partners not only had to store and deliver products, but they also had to enact the sales effort. Its main clients were schools, hospitals, and government institutions, as well as hotels, catering companies, and restaurants.

The company's goal:
This client company intended to launch a loyalty campaign, during a one-year period, that would increase sales through an incentive program based on volume. The company had 29 local partners in the region, each of which had its own sales force. Distributor partners were managed by four sales managers from the company. Volume objectives were set based on past years' performances and the growth potential of each partner;

they had to be defined and agreed upon between the sales manager and the sales director. The company needed to answer this question: What type of incentives should each winning partner receive in exchange for which quantities or volume?

How did they achieve it?
The total sales volume objective for the year was 3,600 tons of product (roughly 10 tons per day); this would represent 30.5% average growth compared to the year before. However, objectives of growth varied widely between partners, ranging from 9% (for some of the older ones) to 71% growth (for those with more potential). The total expected investment was €21,000 without the cost of the incentives, which the company expected would require an investment of around €20,000. The company needed to get a feeling for what this incentive budget should be to make this a sound sales campaign. To do so, marketing and sales ran the project through the prediction stage of the ROI Marketing Matrix model. This generated plausible scenarios for sales, revenues, costs, and profits, allowing the company to define the mix that had the potential to become the most profitable one.

What was the result?
During the validation and prediction stages of any project, there may be several factors you're lacking information about and that will have to actually be measured during execution. In this case, there were two factors that needed to be worked on. One was a variable

under control: the investment in incentives. The other was not under the company's control: the influence of the program on the decision-making process of each distributor. Because there were no precedents, the influence of the program on purchasing was not known and would need to be verified during the execution. Working in the validation stage meant that it was necessary to determine, under the objective of spending close to €20,000 in incentives, how much the loyalty campaign would need to influence sales decision-making to reach breakeven. In other words, given several possible influence scenarios, what would be the investment in incentives that would bring the project to breakeven? Additionally, the company needed to know, based on a combination of these two factors, possible scenarios that would give them the sensitivity needed to make a more educated go-no-go decision.

The actual selling price per ton was €1,333, and based on an operating margin of 5.6%, the company knew it would make €74.67 per ton sold. Since the program was for all the distributors in the region, the company knew that 100% of sales would be impacted by the project, giving them the first isolation factor needed in this case.

Here is what the company calculated:
In order to determine how much to invest in incentives, and in a conservative spirit, it was necessary to consider how various incentive scenarios would impact the profitability of the project. Influence rates were unknown, so the company had to make certain plausible

assumptions. The company decided to have "most likely," "pessimistic," and "optimistic" scenarios that were built by consensus between the sales and marketing departments and general management.

Relating	Acts of purchase impacted by the project?		100%	Expected return	ROI
Validation	Influence of program on purchase decision	for break even scenario	15%	- 0.00	0%
Prediction		Scenario 1: Most likely	20%	12,789.87	5%
Prediction		Scenario 2: Pessimistic	5%	- 27,552.53	-10%
Prediction		Scenario 3: Optimistic	25%	26,237.33	10%

With this validating information in hand, the company knew that if it spent €20,000 in incentives, the program needed to exert an influence of at least 15% on each purchase decision. Was it possible? What did the salespeople think about it? After gathering internal information, they agreed that it was possible to do so, as long as the incentives were good enough to motivate distributors to push the products through all channels.

Now the question turned to a factor that was under the company's control: How much should it invest in incentives? Based on those influence-rate scenarios mentioned before, the company ruled out investment scenarios with the following results:

			Incentives	Expected return	ROI
Relating: prediction	Investment scenario 1	for influence scenario 1		7,790 €	3%
		for influence scenario 2	25,000 € -	32,553 €	-12%
		for influence scenario 3		21,237 €	8%
Relating: prediction	Investment scenario 2	for influence scenario 1		17,790 €	7%
		for influence scenario 2	15,000 € -	22,553 €	-8%
		for influence scenario 3		31,237 €	12%
Relating: prediction	Investment scenario 3	for influence scenario 1	-	7,210 €	-3%
		for influence scenario 2	40,000 € -	47,553 €	-18%
		for influence scenario 3		6,237 €	2%
Relating: validation	Break even investment scenario	for influence scenario 1	32,790 € -	0 €	0%
		for influence scenario 2	- € -	7,553 €	-3%
		for influence scenario 3	46,237 € -	0 €	0%

Conclusions:

With this information, the company concluded that the program could be profitable. For this to happen, it needed to have a plausible influence between 15% and 25% on purchasing decisions. With a €20,000 investment in incentives, there would be an average of €690 in incentives for each partner/distributor. However, the company soon realized that this was too broad and decided to take a deeper look into each partner based on its volume and relative weight.

The company concluded that 42% of the partners – 12 of them – accounted for 75% of sales volume, so it decided to allocate the incentive budget according to this factor. The company created three groups, as follows:

	# of partners in the group	%	Volume	%	Value of incentives	%	Average incentive per partner
Group 1	6	21%	1,943	54%	10,788.45 €	54%	1,798 €
Group 2	6	21%	740	21%	4,108.83 €	21%	685 €
Group 3	17	59%	919	26%	5,102.72 €	26%	300 €
	29		3,602		20,000 €		

Now the average value of incentives (at the starting point of €20,000 investment) was proportional to the sales expectations and would be distributed in a more efficient, results-driven way.

In addition, if the campaign initially appeared not to be having the desired sales effect, and once the influence on purchasing decisions was verified to be between 20% and 25%, the company could increase its investment in incentives by adding between €12,790 and €26,237 (according to the influence exerted) and still not lose money.

- *Functionality 3: Evaluation*

These first two functionalities mentioned so far, validation and prediction, belong to the ROI Marketing Cascade – the phase of the ROI Marketing Matrix dedicated to planning marketing and sales with economic results in mind. During this phase, the organization has not yet invested in the project or campaign, nor has it started execution.

Once the ROI Marketing Cascade has been worked through, it is time to make a go-no-go decision, after which you will start taking action. Acting implies executing the project tasks that trigger the ROI Marketing Ladder, where plans become a reality and the ROI Marketing Matrix deploys its third functionality: evaluation.

The evaluation of a project, the third functionality of sales and marketing economics, takes place during and after its execution. It is linked to the implementation but lasts all the way until the project's period of influence finishes. It is composed of the following steps:

- Data collection
- Relating actual sales and marketing inputs to real business outputs
- Converting outputs to real money
- Calculating the ROI

To carry out data collection, you must follow, step-by-step, the plan developed during the planning phase (the

ROI Marketing Cascade). The deployment of the tools at the right time and to the proper target is key to success. Make sure you validate the data entry frequently during collection in order to avoid planning pitfalls and/or data-collector errors or omissions that could compromise the quality and integrity of the information.

Relating marketing inputs to business outputs is a job based on the relating factors that you previously planned. At this stage, you should be able to determine the number of purchases impacted by the project and the influence that the project had on each purchasing act. This information will give managers the actual impact of the project on sales (the measurement dimension: revenue).

To convert those sales revenues (business output) to monetary value, the evaluator will use the monetary conversion criteria that will assign the value base that will be used for the ROI calculation. For instance, if you established that the gross margin of each car sold in a promotion is $5,000, and the relating factor tells us that the influence of the project (let's say a test drive) is 30% on each impacted purchasing act, we can confidently say that the profit to be attributed to the test drive project is $1,500 for each purchase impacted by the project.

Finally, after converting marketing inputs into business outputs, and having assigned a monetary value to them, we already have all the necessary information to calculate the actual return of our project. We know the costs of the project, and we also know the actual profit generated by it. Calculation is quite simple:

$$\frac{\text{Project benefits}}{\text{Project costs (investment)}} \times 100 = ROI$$

CASE VII: ROI Marketing Management – About ROI Analysis (Evaluation)

Industry: Beverages
Type of organization: Multinational company (Holland)
Offering: B2C

Introduction:
Companies that work in the hotels, restaurants, and cafeterias market (also known as HORECA) have the daunting task of pushing their products through points of sale while generating pull (demand) through marketing efforts. One way of generating traction is by organizing branded events at points of sale, in most cases involving sampling and purchase incentives. At some of these events, product is delivered on consignment and sold during the event. The subject company was running, for the fourth consecutive year, a campaign of 80 events in different cities where it delivered product, POS material, merchandising, glasses, coasters, uniforms for waiters, and everything needed to have a party around its product and brand.

The company's goal:
This company had been working, as a monetary conversion criterion, with a historical margin of €1 per every liter of beverage sold at each event. A new CEO had recently taken over and started wondering where this "historical" margin came from. After internal questioning, nobody could come up with a reasonable

explanation regarding the origin of that calculation. However, everybody had been using that margin as a benchmark. During the previous year's campaign, the company sold 440,000 liters of product; therefore, marketing and sales assumed, and reported, a €440,000 return on the investment. Everybody was happy, and that's why the company kept doing the events. When the CEO decided to hire ROI Marketing Institute for an actual evaluation of the campaign's events to come, faces of disbelief popped up in several meetings.

How did they achieve it?
The objective was to verify whether that historical margin of €1/liter was true or not, and to determine the actual returns per city where the events were being held. Assuming the proper alignment with the company pillars, the team started to prepare the Relating Factors Plan, Monetary Conversion Plan, and Data Collection Plan. The events went on, and at the end of the campaign, the company was able to extract business intelligence and a real figure for the actual return and margin per liter for each event.

What was the result?
The results for only 10 of the 80 cities are shown in the following chart:

City	Total liters sold	Net sales	COGS	Investment	Net return	ROI	Actual margin/lt
1	42,532	€ 88,009	€ 47,324	€ 39,515	€ 1,171	3%	€ 0.03
2	31,000	€ 63,961	€ 34,493	€ 11,087 ✓	€ 18,381	166%	✓ € 0.59
3	25,000	€ 43,476	€ 27,817	€ 32,738 ✗	€ (17,079)	-52%	✗ € (0.68)
4	24,000	€ 49,518	€ 26,704	€ 6,080 ✓	€ 16,734	275%	✓ € 0.70
5	21,500	€ 44,360	€ 23,922	€ 9,254 ✓	€ 11,183	121%	✓ € 0.52
6	17,000	€ 32,570	€ 18,915	€ 35,549 ✗	€ (21,894)	-62%	✗ € (1.29)
7	14,160	€ 36,817	€ 15,755	€ 25,252	€ (4,190)	-17%	€ (0.30)
8	13,000	€ 38,318	€ 14,465	€ 9,406 ✓	€ 14,446	154%	✓ € 1.11
9	12,000	€ 24,759	€ 13,352	€ 2,398 ✓	€ 9,009	376%	✓ € 0.75
10	12,000	€ 24,759	€ 13,352	€ 9,916	€ 1,491	15%	€ 0.12

Conclusions:

Results were quite diverse. In the case of the actual profit per liter, it ranged from -€82.07 per liter to €1.90 per liter. A full and thorough review of each and every event became mandatory. Why were there so many money-losing events? Out of the 80, only seven events made a profit of between €0.95 per liter and €1.05 per liter; 35 events were losing money (€181,000 in total) and 45 were making money (€156,000 in total). The overall ROI of the whole campaign was -4.65%.

It became evident that return-based management is good, as long as it is executed properly. If done wrong, things can get much worse, and they usually do.

Taking "historical" data for granted is fine as long as you know and trust the source. In addition, you should also understand the nature, origin, and math behind all figures. Do not take anything for granted!

- *Functionality 4: Planning*

As previously mentioned, calculating ROI is not the final stop on your profitability trip. A thorough analysis of the correlation and causation of impacts will lead to a set of conclusions and recommendations that can reveal the need for corrective actions and/or improve results in the future. Once you have calculated the ROI of a project, and based on the results of that calculation, you will end up with six different types of measures:

   a. Positioning measures
   b. Education measures
   c. Interactions
   d. Costs
   e. Revenues
   f. Return

Some of these measures will have already translated into real cash flow, and some of them will have not. But those that have not been translated (sometimes the cost and the time to isolate the contribution of certain intangibles may be too high or take too long to make it feasible) should not go to waste. All these indicators mark the opening of the last functionality of the ROI Marketing Matrix: Planning.

Planning is the fourth functionality of the ROI Marketing Matrix and, I daresay, of any method or system to evaluate the economic contribution of any sales and/or marketing project.

Planning refers to the series of efforts made to extract business intelligence from each and every evaluation cycle. It is obvious that obtaining a clear, robust, and credible ROI figure is relevant for any organization. But the benefits of deploying a monitoring system at the market and business levels don't stop there. After completing an evaluation, you will have in hand a full range of quantitative and qualitative data that will help you plan future projects in a much more accurate way and with less uncertainty.

Some of these indicators are:

- Interaction conversion ratios
- Education impact ratios
- Positioning evolution ratios
- Cost per unit (of activity or result)
- Revenue conversion ratios
- Return on investment
- Cost/benefit ratio
- Activity break-even point
- Response ratios
- Etc.

All these indicators will help decision-makers to have unbiased criteria for evaluation, to objectively estimate the potential outcome of future projects, to have a common standard to compare projects that are of completely different nature, to better negotiate budgets, to know the opportunity cost of any given project, to plan based on economic results (rather than on activity execution), and more.

Decision-makers have already analyzed data, extracting actionable information that can be translated into more- and better-informed business decisions. In the middle of this process, you will most likely need to add some technological processes. After collecting information from internal and external sources, you will need to prepare the data for analysis, develop and run queries, extract conclusions, and report to decision-makers (often with control panels, dashboards, and/or software for data visualization). This is when the convergence between marketing, sales, and IT departments becomes paramount to extracting the most out of experience and implementation (marketing and sales operations).

When projects are methodologically evaluated and sales, marketing, and IT work in a convergent way, something magical happens:

- Attrition between departments is reduced.
- Performance is determined by data, rather than by impressions and/or subjective criteria.
- Sales, marketing, and IT departments plan, work, and monitor results in an aligned way.
- Resources are shared and more productively used.
- Business results improve.
- Sales becomes marketing-driven and marketing becomes sales-driven.
- IT becomes much more than an optimization tool.

For this convergence to happen, organizations must create liaison positions and/or components that can facilitate such convergence. These could take the shape of a business data analyst, a multidisciplinary committee, or even an external consulting firm that can work on the alignment until this convergence becomes standard. It may take some time, but the results are totally worth it – and the reward is also financial (hopefully for the company as marginal profits and for personnel as an extra bonus).

It works like this: Next time the organization sets the objectives for a future marketing or sales project, it will already have a relating factor to define the influence of positioning on customers' purchase decision-making, as well as for the influence of education on such decisions. It will also already have a conversion ratio for the impact of interactions on revenue streams, a cost benchmark, and a past measure of actual return to use as an indicator for a return objective. Having all this business intelligence at a glance, managers will be able to make better and much more educated decisions when planning. It will also provide impartial conditions to comparatively evaluate future projects.

Once objectives are set using this knowledge, decision-makers will also have monetary conversion criteria set as the baseline to convert whichever indicator is isolated to profits.

Furthermore, after execution, and once the data collection process is finished (for which managers will also have a benchmark), evaluators will be able to define how many purchases were impacted by the project and the influence of the overall project on those purchases. The overall process of defining the relating factors and monetary conversion criteria – which at the beginning might have looked complex – is now part of the process. There is no need to go back and generate them and find consensus, as that was done the first time and only needs to be revalidated about once a year, or every other year.

Another direct consequence of knowing the actual economic return of sales and marketing projects is that the marketing budget will be able to be managed as an investment portfolio based on profitability. This puts marketing and sales efforts right below and supporting the bottom line of the business – a strategic position.

CASE VIII: ROI Marketing Management – About Business Intelligence (Planning)

Industry: Finance and Insurance
Type of organization: Multinational company (Spain)
Offering: B2C

Introduction:
The financial services industry is a complex one, requiring not only a good set of skills and knowledge, but also an in-depth understanding of and capability to use and control technological evolution and disruption in a way that does not change the essence of the business or alter compliance.

New ways of consumption (Cabify, Uber, Airbnb, etc.) created the need of new products and services in an environment that is not completely regulated yet.

Additionally, when it comes to choosing a communication and purchase channel, clients behave unpredictably; customer journeys are quite erratic, if not undecipherable. The concept of "omni-channel" has taken off, but no company figured out how best to take advantage of it. Client recruiting, retention, cross-selling, and recovering, as well as all the customer-journey phases discussed earlier in this book (consideration, evaluation, purchase, experience, and loyalty) can happen either at a physical point of sale or through a call center, mobile applications, online channels, dedicated web pages, sales reps and agents, etc.

Companies struggle, with very low rates of success, to decipher this customer journey map in a way that allows them to track efficiency and optimization. Conversion became the term of choice when it comes to reporting. But reporting on conversion still remains fuzzy, and it is not robust enough to generate internal credibility.

This was the challenge this Spanish multinational faced for years and was determined to resolve.

The company's goal:
The company needed to generate an attribution model that would allow it to evaluate and track actions such as recruiting, retention, cross-selling, recovering, and loyalty. It needed to track different (from the profitability point of view) client segments and consider a broad range of communication channels (web, call center, own points of sale, and external agent network).

The idea was to generate a decision-making matrix (see the following matrix) that would use profitability (ROI) as the performance indicator. The matrix would be based on a combination of client segment, type of sales action, and communication channel or channels used for the campaign. With this matrix, managers could more efficiently manage sales campaigns with an eye towards profitability rather than on interactions (mainly service underwriting at that time).

The business intelligence generated from several cycles of evaluation would diminish the margin of error and the risks involving blind implementation based on conversion only.

Impact (ROI) matrix based on channel and client segment

Type of action	Recruiting				Cross-selling				Retention				Loyalty				Recovering			
Channel/client segment	Gold	Silver	Bronze	Iron	Gold	Silver	Bronze	Iron	Gold	Silver	Bronze	Iron	Gold	Silver	Bronze	Iron	Gold	Silver	Bronze	Iron
Web													1%							
Emailing		14%			1%	12%	15%	41%	43%					-12%			32%			
SMS	11%		-18%			-17%				3%			4%		11%			8%		
Postal mailing				22%						2%				7%		-5%				
Call center		15%			10%	25%	30%	35%	-34%				23%					12%		
Point of sales	9%		17%								-22%			-13%						-12%
Agents network																6%				

How did they achieve it?
The main problem was to build credibility around an attribution model that could assign value to each channel, for each type of client, depending on the sales goal of the activity.

This company in particular has more than 35 million clients in more than 100 countries. A robust Data Collection Plan could ensure that the model considered market particularities, but first it was necessary to test whether the model delivered the expected decision-making business intelligence. Validating the model implied running a pilot project in one country first, then translating it into a standard procedure through systems. After that, the company could begin considering deployment at an international level. These are the steps of the overall plan:

- Model development (pillars, objectives, plans, and ROI Sensitivity Analysis)

- Simulator (non-working environment) test with data from real cases
- Pilot test (working environment) with data from real cases
- Model validation
- Adjustment and/or translation of the model into the company's systems (ERP, CRM, etc.)
- First country training deployment
- Three-country simulator and pilot tests for model validation
- Adjustment and/or translation of the model into the country systems for country customization
- Deployment in other countries

What was the result?
At the time of publishing this book, the project was still ongoing. The simulator worked, and the company conducted a training program for internal leaders to ensure implementation and optimization. The model represents a step up on strategic sales and marketing planning. It brought together at the same table 11 different departments for a single program, with common performance indicators and a direct impact on the bottom line of the business, all working in a convergent way.

Conclusions:
Sometimes cases may look difficult, and the overwhelming complexity of reality may lead you to believe that some quests might even be impossible. In this case, the key to success was, and still is, that all

departments work in an aligned and convergent way with common metrics and goals and with an overall business view, rather than a compartmental, skewed scope.

CASE IX: ROI Marketing Management – About Using Marketing Economics for Sales Purposes

Industry: Events
Type of organization: Government
                               (City Council, Switzerland)

Introduction:
What happens when a city council wants to bring in a huge international sports event that will put the town in front of millions of spectators through media exposure and broadcasting? How can the city decide how much is too much to pay for the rights to have such a great marketing opportunity? This is the case of a city in Switzerland that wanted to host an event, for which it had to pay a very high fee. This is an event project (hence a marketing project) that had the purpose of "selling" the city for tourism during and after the event. The figures in this case are not real, nor are they adjusted to market, but they serve to portray the case and the relevance of the topic.

The organization's goal:
To have strong arguments to negotiate with the world sports federation for the fees it would need to pay in order to host the event in the city. The stakes were high, as the fees to pay just for the right to host the event were around 3 million francs. These fees did not include all the investments the city needed to make in order to host the event, such as preparing practice facilities,

improving city services and roads, providing security, etc. – estimated to be around 2 million francs. In addition, non-paid utilities consumption, cleaning during the event, city personnel and employee overtime during the event, and the extra services to be provided to the organization represented another 3 million francs. The question was: Is it worth it to invest 8 million francs to host the event? If not, in which conditions would it be worthwhile?

How did they achieve it?
This case is about the financial validation of a marketing project. The city council needed to know the profit and loss account of the event in order to validate a go-no-go decision. The city knew that the event would portray the city to the world (positioning), incoming and potential tourists would have the opportunity to learn about what the city had to offer (education), tourists would visit (interaction), tourists and athletes would spend money in the city (revenues), and the investment (costs) would deliver surpluses (returns) to improve the quality of life of its inhabitants.

The city knew how it wanted to portray itself and what to offer to tourists, and it set the objective of receiving at least 150,000 tourists during the three days the event would last. Each tourist was expected to stay at least three nights, spending 250 francs per night on hotels, 120 francs per day on food, and 200 francs per stay on other goods.

What was the result?

The city worked thoroughly to determine the exact financial value that these 150,000 expected tourists would bring to it. This value could be calculated in several ways, including but not limited to: income from taxes and municipal fees, increase in garbage collection fees, fines and tickets, etc. Word of mouth and media exposure could add to this value through people coming and spending money in the city after the event because they either saw it on TV or in media, or they were recommended to come by somebody who was there for the event. The city decided, for the sake of conservative reasoning, not to consider this last incremental value generation, which would be difficult to verify; instead, it focused only on the cash flows from visitors to the event. With this in mind, they came up with a figure very close to the investment of 8 million francs. As previously seen, coming too close to breakeven should force managers to reconsider execution and do a thorough revision of the economics of the project. In this particular case, the city could come up with two possible options: The city could obtain the rights to extend the event with extra content for two or three more days without additional fees (increasing the spending per visitor and revenues). Alternatively, the sports federation could reduce the fees or link them to the actual number of visitors that came for the event, making it variable and diminishing the risks.

Conclusions:
In this case, working through the economics of a marketing project helped an organization to renegotiate, with a strong argument, the fees for an incoming event of interest that could bring benefits to residents. This is very similar to most sponsorship cases, when validation not only serves to help make go-no-go decisions, but also to negotiate and aim for profits before investing.

Summary bullets:

- Use the ROI Marketing Matrix to its full extent. It is not just about calculating the ROI or projects.

- Validate your projects prior to investment.

- Make educated and objective go-no-go decisions. Do not make them based on gut feeling or what everybody likes (or liked in the past).

- Try out possible outcome scenarios based on variables under control.

- Plan your work, then work your plan.

- Make sure you not only have a positive or negative result, but also a set of data that you will be able to use in the future – continuously improving the planning and decision-making process.

Chapter V:
Is My Organization Ready to Manage Sales & Marketing Projects for Profit?

I am confident that at this point you already know how far your organization is from being able to implement an ROI Marketing management model. Most people should already know, at this point, if their company really evaluates sales and marketing projects from an economic point of view. Most also probably know what they still need in order to be able to measure the actual return of their marketing and sales expenditures.

In any case, adopting a management model is a strategic decision, which must be based on a solid diagnosis and have clear objectives with accountable goals. If you want to give a push to this initiative, regardless of whether you are at a strategic decision-making level or reporting to one, you will need to establish an early assessment that can tell your organization how far it is from being able to implement such a management model. Certain indicators can define how far an organization is from determining the actual return of its sales and marketing investments. The following figure portrays different degrees of alignment with this management model; these degrees can facilitate a deeper approach to it.

Chart 6: Organization ROI Marketing Alignment

Each degree of alignment represents the degree to which a company's marketing management model does or does not take marketing and sales profitability into account. Let's see what each degree means and actions that can be taken from your side if you wish to start moving towards an ROI Marketing management model.

Levels of Organization ROI Marketing Alignment

- *Alignment Level #1: No systematic performance measurement*

This level of alignment represents an organization in which sales and marketing are issues of low concern, either because it is a very successful business (so it doesn't need to worry about selling) or because its management is highly risk-taking. In either case, this is a dangerous situation. By the time the negative behaviors (either internal or external) impact the organization, it will be too late to act, and the damage will be done. In this case, marketing and sales campaigns are not planned; they are executed depending on available cash at hand and/or as a reaction to a market move or an internal need. There is no such thing as a marketing budget, and instead of being planned, marketing and sales expenditures are done at the discretion of the decision-maker. This is typical of small businesses, fast-growing startups, or monopolies.

How can you begin changing such a business? The first step is to generate awareness around the issue and relevance of measuring, planning, and executing marketing and sales projects with consideration for their economic impact. Decision-makers (even in small businesses) should see that these two disciplines have a direct impact on the bottom line and realize that proactively planning and executing is much better than managing by reacting, which implies higher risks. The best way to generate awareness is to introduce the issue by attending conferences and training courses, collecting and sharing reading material, studying and showing best practices, and bringing the issue to the table whenever needed. Introduce the concern.

- *Alignment Level #2: Systematic marketing and sales performance measurement*

Believe it or not, this second stage, very low on the scale, is where most multinational and large corporations are. These types of organizations usually have large marketing, communications, and sales departments that have measurement systems and resources to collect data at several levels. ERPs (enterprise resource planning systems) and CRMs (customer relationship management systems) are the most common tools used for this purpose, together with a large cluster of riggings for gathering analytics from digital and online interactions. In addition, these companies count on a large pool of suppliers that regularly report on their own services' performance (questionable data, at least). However, in all cases, performance indicators refer only to marketing and sales inputs. They report on attendees to an event, registrations, unique visitors to a webpage, new distributors, new leads, opportunity stages, etc. All these indicators are not the result of the campaigns they come from, but the inputs that those projects and campaigns generate. These inputs go to a business impact that is never measured, to a cause-effect relationship that is never found, to a business output that is never linked.

Although these organizations have large budgets, in most cases those budgets are assigned based on the previous year's overall business performance. They are limited by, and satisfy, financial planning and needs. In all cases, budgets are an adjustable variable: If sales are down or below expectations, marketing and sales budgets are often cut and plans shrunk.

How do you affect change in such a business? In this case, decision-makers are most likely aware of what they are missing. They know they lack a vision of the impact on the business of their sales and marketing performance, and that is why they see marketing as a tactical activity, instead of a strategic one with uncertain impact in value and time. Decision-makers do not know that marketing and sales projects can be evaluated in a robust and credible way. In other words, they need to know that it can be done and that there are tools and methodologies (like the ROI Marketing Matrix) available to do it. Collecting and introducing information about the issue, available training, options to try, costs, and deployment are some of the steps that can be taken.

- *Alignment Level #3: Correlation between marketing inputs and business outputs*

I once had a multinational client in Spain that was at this level (as are many multinational businesses around the world). The idea of generating correlations between marketing spending and sales variations is tempting, and in a way, not broadly incorrect. However, making correlations can be tricky, as correlation does not mean causation.

It all starts with measuring market penetration and sales volume evolution before, during, and after the project and/or campaign (also known as baseline lift). Then a company infers that, if all other conditions are the same, the variation was due to the marketing or sales investment. Then comes the first question: The same as what? The same period of last year? Last quarter? Isolating in this way requires working with two methods: control groups and trend line analysis.

There is one very common mistake (which my Spanish client didn't commit): not discounting market evolution. If, for instance, after the campaign, sales grew by 20% but the overall market grew by 25%, then the campaign didn't grow sales; on the contrary, sales shrunk by 5% during the campaign.

Correlation does not mean causation. A correlation coefficient is non-parametric and simply indicates that two variables are somehow linked with each other; it does not represent any kind of relationship. Regression models can help managers investigate bivariate and multivariate relationships. Let's take the following chart, obtained from tylervigen.com (a fun website where you will see lots of other cases with factoids and spurious charts):

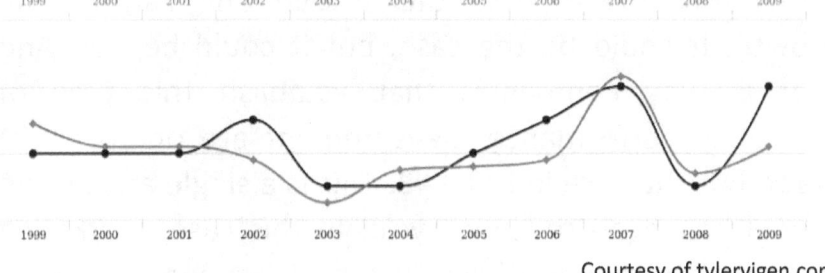

Courtesy of tylervigen.com

If you see this chart, you can be tempted to think that these two variables are related to each other. In fact, they have a 66.6% correlation. However, they show two completely unrelated events. The black line shows the number of movies Nicolas Cage appeared in, and the grey line shows the number of people who drowned by falling into a pool in the United States. All the data comes from reputable sources (Internet Movie Database and Centers for Disease Control and Prevention). But neither of these two factors (which are correlated and from reputable sources) can justify the government of the United States requiring more lifeguards and buoyancy devices at pools every time a Nicolas Cage movie is in theaters. In fact, these two factors may correlate to each other due to what is called a spurious relationship: something they have in common, that affects them both, but that doesn't mean that they influence each other. In this case, it might be that Nicolas Cage's movies are released during the summer, when most pool drownings occur.

Going back to sales and marketing projects, the fact that sales grow during and after an investment does not necessarily mean that the investment caused the growth. It could be the case, but it could be not. And that is why companies that establish this type of economic performance measurement are on the right track, but they are in Level #3. This is a single attribution model based on revenue cycle. In this case, marketing budgets are planned based on past economic impacts inferred from sales and marketing correlations. Although it does not determine a go-no-go decision-making process, neither is it robust enough to have managers plan sales and marketing activities as an investment or work with revenue cycle projections. It is a higher stage of planning with the implicit risk of discovering, when it is already too late, that the correlation did not mean causation.

- *Alignment Level #4: Assumption of marketing impact on business output variations*

This level represents an evolution from Level #3, because it means that a cause-effect relationship is assumed by certain criteria. The criteria need to be robust, accepted by all reporting levels, and work based on a multi-touch attribution model – meaning that they do not consider the project as the sole cause of sales variations, and other projects and factors (as many as possible) are included in the equation and credited. Organizations at this level are frequently those that use standard attribution models in digital marketing, such as time decay or customer journey (also known as full-path attribution). All attribution models in digital marketing are based on a set of criteria that are accepted and considered standard. In this case, marketing is planned based on the measured effectiveness and return calculated through these attribution models. Several channels, media, and tools are considered, making a more efficient marketing mix management. However, as previously mentioned, the attribution is based on assumptions that are generally accepted, but not robust enough to make companies treat sales and marketing budgets as investments. There is still a risk that assumptions might be skewed or wrong. In other cases, these attribution models are based on "secret algorithms" or black boxes created by the channel or medium as a way to measure its own performance. And believe it or not, few multinational businesses use them as a standard!

- *Alignment Level #5: Causation between business and sales and marketing impact*

At this level, robustness must be guaranteed. It means that there is a more scientific intervention that determines the cause-effect relationship between the project and/or campaign and its impact on business. This is the first level that uses a true revenue-based model. It is more than a correlation, and it is defined by an attribution model that has very little room for error. Of course, not all projects can fall into this category of measurement. But companies that plan and execute sales and marketing projects based on this causation model not only have a higher probability of economic success, but they also have better and more solid management support for marketing, higher expectations, and better commitment from the salesforce. At this level, marketing and sales efforts become strategic, top management is involved and reported to, and go-no-go decisions are based on business impact rather than on marketing achievements, gut feeling, internal sympathy with the project, etc.

Redemption and loyalty programs are especially visible in this type of organization, and, in general, in all those projects where traceability and customer journeys are unequivocally defined.

- *Alignment Level #6: Systematic approach to measuring marketing and sales impact on business*

This level represents an evolution from Level #5. Organizations at Level #6 have put in place standard processes and procedures that help managers plan, execute, and monitor projects using causation- and revenue-based attribution models. It implies the adoption of a model that is translated into systems and tools that facilitate its execution. Planning based on revenue generation becomes methodological, and sales and marketing work together towards common goals. Very few organizations work at this level.

- *Alignment Level #7: Planning using economic evaluation of sales and marketing projects*

Going up in evolution towards business impact are those organizations that, on top of having a systematic approach to measuring actual revenue from sales and marketing projects, include a return evaluation when planning future projects, campaigns, and overall sales and marketing plans. This is done sporadically and outside of the systems, but it shows that profit is a concern, beyond revenue. It implies jumping to a higher level, from sales to business management. It means that managers are managing for profit, and that sales and marketing speak the language of business, rather than one that is valid only in their own departments.

- *Alignment Level #8: ROI measurement as a standard procedure*

At this level, the concerns raised in Level #7 have been incorporated into the systematic approach of Level #6. Return calculations are done regularly and inside of a system. They represent milestones in the system and one of its deliverable results. Being at this level implies that organizations have developed an entire return-based management model to its final stage. Although it is not common to see this type of organization, most companies are trying to aim high and get as close as possible. Employee turnover, personal interests, and internal pressure (or lack thereof) are the most common barriers to reaching this level. But you can rest assured that most general managers and C-level executives have this level on their wish lists and in the back of their minds.

- *Alignment Level #9: ROI reporting at executive level*

This level not only shows that the company has developed and put in place a return-based management model that is systematically managed standard, but also that top management is aware of the model and believes in it.

A very large Dutch multinational client once called us to review a marketing management model that was put in place by a large multinational consulting firm. The company invested millions of euros in the model and trained the organization at a global scale. Years later, the company discovered that very few people were using the system, and top management did not even receive reports on its outputs. In fact, there were actually no outputs! The whole model was not completely operational and, furthermore, it did not deliver results that were worth the interest of top executives.

When a system delivers results that are worth reporting on and that general management and top executives pay attention to, it represents a model that speaks the language of business in a robust and credible way. This allows top management to make strategic decisions based on it.

- *Alignment Level #10: Strategic planning, including ROI as a KPI*

The top level of the organization ROI Marketing alignment scale not only reports to top management using a systematic approach of a return-based sales and marketing model, but it is also capable of extracting business intelligence that will help managers plan future projects. The whole system becomes a planning, monitoring, and reporting tool. Companies in this level send a clear message to stakeholders and shareholders, shouting out loud that the organization treats sales and marketing budgets as investments rather than as expenses. Shareholders will be happy to see the extent to which the company can seek profits representing their interest, analysts will be comfortable with this exercise of rigor about which they can only talk positively, investors will increase their willingness to pay for better and more efficient management, and more. At this level, marketing and sales projects have an accepted opportunity cost and budgets are managed as an investment portfolio.

- *Moving through the alignment levels*

Based on past experiences, the whole process to go from Level #1 to Level #10 can take approximately three to four years, depending on the complexity of the organization, including its product range, distribution channels, and complexity and length of its sales cycle. Smaller companies and those with narrower product ranges can do it much faster.

For a deeper vision of your organization's current alignment, you can go to goo.gl/396Mm6 and fill out the ROI Marketing Survey. Once you've completed it, make sure you <u>get the final scoring of your questionnaire and email that result through the contact form at</u> roimarketinginstitute.com/contact; you will receive a free diagnosis fact sheet from ROI Marketing Institute. It will indicate the current situation of your organization compared to others and offer a set of recommendations to start your quest towards a profitable marketing management model.

While working to define, test, and implement a return-based management model for sales and marketing activities, most organizations will find themselves in a back-and-forth process that brings up issues and discussions about what profit is, how value is determined and assigned, and how performance is measured. At the beginning, this process might look complex and not free from debate. But this debate is constructive and helps to build convergence between sales, marketing, and IT. Those companies that have already gone down this road are still benefiting from it. Those that have not (the majority, unfortunately) are always taking risks that can be managed and avoided. Like most models, it is seldom a definitive one. Especially considering the speed at which markets, and consumer behaviors, are changing. The relating factors and monetization criteria of today must be reviewed and validated at least every other year. Shareholders' priorities might change, stakeholders' management can be altered, and businesses also evolve at an unprecedented speed. So, don't feel distressed if you have to start with ratios and criteria with which you are not completely comfortable. It is always good to start with modest aims; after all, it is better to start on a path towards marketing and sales profitability than to not start at all. As you run evaluation cycles, they will improve in accuracy and robustness, hence, in credibility. Walking your way through the alignment scale will facilitate embracement and deployment.

During our years of helping companies and organizations define their paths to and deploy a return-based management model, ROI Marketing Institute developed the Roadmap to ROI found on the next page.

Chart 7: ROI Marketing Roadmap

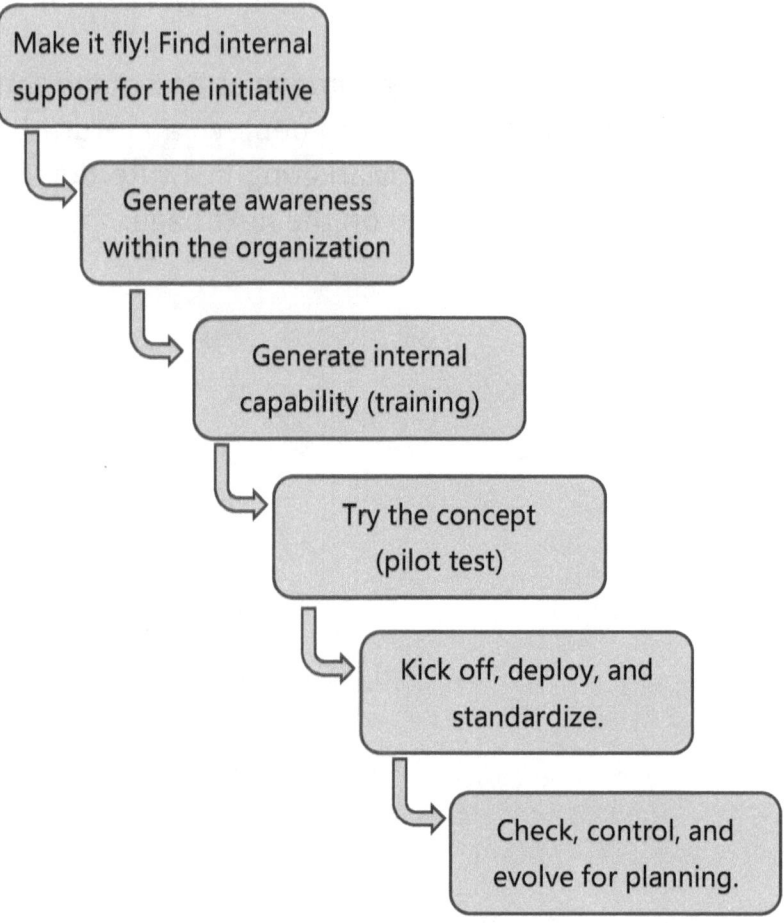

With this roadmap in hand, and by deploying a return-based sales and marketing management model, managers and decision-makers should never be afraid of obtaining negative results, but they should be afraid of not having results at all. Sale people and marketers are not responsible for decisions made without needed relevant information. Initially, in most cases, lack of information is the main cause of an unprofitable project.

If you don't know how other projects performed financially in the past, it is difficult to plan future projects for profitable results. You cannot judge past decisions using today's information. By the same token, you cannot obtain different results by going through the same process over and over. So, embrace a new, innovative, return-based sales and marketing model. There is a lot to gain!

If you have this book in your hands and have read all the way through it, you are one step closer to making obsolete John Wanamaker's epitaph phrase: "Half the money I spend on advertising is wasted; the trouble is I don't know which half." Now you can know!

Chapter VI:
About Stakeholder Management – Another Intangible Worth Measuring

We all know that marketing is about managing and communicating the attributes and intangibles of products and services that generate value to the customer; in exchange, the customer pays a price from which the company generates a profit.

The challenge, as presented in this book in the case of marketing, lies in making the intangible accountable in terms of real economic impact on the bottom line of any given organization. Soft measures like "excellent" to "very poor" scaling can only speak about the quality of a relationship in a relative way. They do not provide any clue as to how the relationship impacts the P&L of the business, nor do they give any clue about whether the amount of money that is about to be invested in a marketing project is too little, enough, or too much.

Brand awareness, reputation, and marketing concepts, in general, are not the only intangibles that generate real economic value for an organization. Sustainability programs, training, and stakeholder management also create value for an organization, and this value needs to be measured. Not everything that counts can be counted, just as not everything that can be counted counts.

Since R. Edward Freeman published his book *Strategic Management: A Stakeholder Approach* (1984), the issue of stakeholder management has been at the top of managers' agendas. Most literature and research written about stakeholder management theory is based on determining how to classify and measure the quality of these relationships and how to plan actions to favor its improvement. In all cases, planning for stakeholder management should not only be about defining how to engage in activities or interactions with them, but it should also be about planning how to generate value for both stakeholders and the organization. In other words, it should be a plan about achieving certain results: a specific set of measurable goals that have both tangible (economic) and intangible impacts.

What Defines a Stakeholder for Your Organization?

There is nothing worse than planning stakeholder management without a proper definition of what and who the main stakeholders are. A stakeholder is a person, group of persons, or organization that has interests and/or concerns that can be affected by the organization's activities and interactions. For such a person or group to be considered a stakeholder, the activities and interactions of this person, group, or organization must also be able to influence the interests and concerns of the organization. Although this may seem an obvious definition, the fact that the interaction could affect both parties is of the essence.

Who Are Your Stakeholders, Specifically?

Once it is clear that the interests and concerns of both parties are affected, the way in which the relationship affects the organization will define segmentation criteria to determine clustering for proper planning. For this purpose, it is important to identify the interactions and how they are leveraged with or between stakeholders. Those leverages are: power, claims, and influence. On one side of the equation, there will always be a power relationship: who affects whom and in what way. On the other side are the demands that, based on that power relationship, will determine the extent (small or big) and tone (positive or negative) of the interactions' impact. Additionally, there are stakeholders that do not have a specific claim, but that can exert influence on the extent and tone of other stakeholders' relationships. These last two issues – extent and tone of impact – represent the two primary criteria of any classification. In the middle between power and demands there is always a "stake" – an aspect that is at risk, that can be lost or diminished, and that one of the parties needs to address for the other (or themselves) to avoid harm. In a broader sense, for every person, group, and organization that is a stakeholder in a company, the extent and degree of the impact generated by the interactions that affect them will define whether that relationship needs to be taken care of or not. This will establish the threshold between what is and what is not a stakeholder from then on.

There are several other ways to define and classify stakeholders. Ronald K. Mitchell, Bradley R. Agle, and Donna J. Wood created a very accurate chronology of the definition of a stakeholder in their paper published in 1997:

Who Is a Stakeholder? A Chronology (Mitchell, Agle, and Wood)

Author(s)	Definition
Stanford memo, 1963	"those groups without whose support the organization would cease to exist" (cited in Freeman & Reed, 1983, and Freeman, 1984)
Rhenman, 1964	"are depending on the firm in order to achieve their personal goals and on whom the firm is depending for its existence" (cited in Nasi, 1995)
Ahlstedt & Jahnukainen, 1971	"driven by their own interests and goals are participants in a firm, and thus depending on it and whom for its sake the firm is depending" (cited in Nasi, 1995)
Freeman & Reed, 1983	Wide: "can affect the achievement of an organization's objectives or who is affected by the achievement of an organization's objectives;" Narrow: "on which the organization is dependent for its continued survival"
Freeman, 1984	"can affect or is affected by the achievement of the organization's objectives"
Freeman & Gilbert, 1987	"can affect or is affected by a business"
Cornell & Shapiro, 1987	"claimants" who have "contracts"
Evan & Freeman, 1988	"have a stake in or claim on the firm"
Evan & Freeman, 1988	"benefit from or are harmed by, and whose rights are violated or respected by, corporate actions"

Bowie, 1988	"without whose support the organization would cease to exist"
Alkhafaji, 1989	"groups to whom the corporation is responsible"
Carroll, 1989	"asserts to have one or more of these kinds of stakes;" "ranging from an interest to a right (legal or moral) to ownership or legal title to the company's assets or property"
Freeman & Evan, 1990	"contract holders"
Thompson et al., 1991	in "relationship with an organization"
Savage et al., 1991	"have an interest in the actions of an organization and ... the ability to influence it"
Hill & Jones, 1992	"constituents who have a legitimate claim on the firm ... established through 133 the existence of an exchange relationship" who supply "the firm with critical resources (contributions) and in exchange each expects its interests to be satisfied (by inducements)"
Brenner, 1993	"having some legitimate, non-trivial relationship with an organization [such as] exchange transactions, action impacts, and moral responsibilities"
Carroll, 1993	"asserts to have one or more of the kinds of stakes in business"
Freeman, 1994	participants in "the human process of joint value creation"
Wicks et al., 1994	"interact with and give meaning and definition to the corporation"
Langtry, 1994	the firm is significantly responsible for their well-being, or they hold a moral or legal claim on the firm
Starik, 1994	"can and are making their actual stakes known;" "are or might be influenced by, or are or potentially are influencers of, some organization"
Clarkson, 1994	"bear some form of risk as a result of having invested some form of capital, human or financial, something of value, in a firm" or "are placed at risk as a result of a firm's activities"

Clarkson, 1995	"have, or claim, ownership, rights, or interests in a corporation and its activities"
Nasi, 1995	"interact with the firm and thus make its operation possible"
Brenner, 1995	"are or which could impact or be impacted by the firm/organization"
Donaldson & Preston, 1995	"persons or groups with legitimate interests in procedural and/or substantive aspects of corporate activity"

Several authors point to salience, urgency, and legitimacy (Mitchell); at power to unlock the use of resources (Pfeffer & Salancik); at multiplicity (Oliver), attributes, and type of relationship; or internal and external to the organization as ways to classify stakeholders. There are other visions that look into the essential-transactional (employees, customers, and suppliers) or non-essential-transactional (associations, government) nature of the relationship. Wartick and Cochran suggest looking at the relationship with stakeholders based on the response policy needed to deal with them: reactive (deny responsibility), defensive (admit responsibility but fight for it), accommodative (accept responsibility), or proactive (accept responsibility).

What Is the Influence of Stakeholders on Your Organization?

Generating segmentation criteria serves the purpose of defining the influence of stakeholders on the organization or business. When considering clustering, and adhering to the concept of visualizing the economic impact of these relationships, you may consider the following criteria to classify stakeholders: impact on business and visibility.

Impact on business means any activity or interaction generated by a stakeholder that increases the operating cost of the business (fines, insurance, preventive maintenance, etc.), or that affects, in any way, the business's income-generation capability (sales, savings, cost avoidance, etc.). The ability to influence real cash inflows and outflows determines the degree of impact that the relationship with the stakeholder has on the organization and its relevance from a bottom-line perspective. In several industries (such as telecommunications, food, automotive, finance, and energy), regulatory bodies are an extremely relevant and impactful stakeholder that can very quickly drive profits and businesses from likely and viable to unlikely and unsuccessful. Employees and unions are another example of very impactful stakeholders for the economics of the business.

Visibility is represented by the ability of stakeholders' activities and interactions to be seen by other stakeholders. This criterion is very relevant when the scope of the impact goes beyond the single stakeholder and can spread to others. Everybody, especially in a business environment, is very aware of the power of communication and social media to spread a message. Non-governmental and nonprofit organizations also serve the purpose of raising awareness about illegal activities, as well as environmental and social impact. This further increases the pressure on companies to manage all three dimensions of sustainability: economic, social, and environmental. Former U.S. Vice President Al Gore once said, "If it can be known, it will be known." Abundant examples (child labor, pollution, damaging natural resources, etc.) prove that perceptions about certain issues, whether accurate or not, can have a deep impact on an organization's bottom line. The ability to reach other stakeholders is the real source of power for communication media and some other stakeholders, such as unions, NGOs, and industry associations.

Seeing the relationship with stakeholders in terms of their impact on business and visibility puts the focus on what generates value to the business, in direct relation to the concerns and interests of the stakeholder. The combination of these two aspects will clearly define the stakeholder's salience, relevance, and the urgency of responding to their claims and requests. It will also allow an organization to plan proactively how to relate to the stakeholder. Once an organization is able to define the persons, groups of persons, and organizations that can affect the bottom line and spread their messages (while being affected by the activities and interactions of the organization), stakeholder managers should focus on defining the value-drivers for both stakeholders and the organization.

What Is the Influence of Your Organization on Each Stakeholder?

I'll begin with the assumption that business value-drivers include a positive impact on the bottom line, as well as a constructive influence on the company's positioning (the way stakeholders think about it) and education (the knowledge the organization wants to transmit to stakeholders). With that in mind, stakeholder managers should focus on what each group of stakeholders would consider to be positive and negative influences. In this case, it is necessary to work stakeholder by stakeholder, as the interest of one group will not necessarily coincide with the concerns of others. In the case of an energy company, for instance, its cooperation with UNICEF focusing on the education of children to minimize environmental impact will vastly differ from the interest motivating a governing political party's decision about installing a renewable-energy power plant. In addition, for many stakeholders, most value-drivers are not economic, adding more complexity to stakeholder management.

Most organizations have common groups of stakeholders, which might include employees, customers, media, suppliers, regulatory bodies, industry associations, and universities. In almost all cases there will always be particular groups linked to a specific business. For example, landowners will always be stakeholders in the case of industries needing to install temporary facilities like antennas for the telecommunications industry or windmill generators for renewable-energy businesses.

Each stakeholder has its own value drivers. Once those drivers are defined, stakeholder managers should determine the tone of impact the business exerts on their interests, whether it is positive or negative, and the degree of such influence. By determining the tone of impact, stakeholder managers will be able to increase or decrease impacts. By determining the degree of such influence on a scale of tangential to indispensable, they will be able to determine power leverage. To define those drivers, it is useful to categorize the types of interests and way of thinking behind each group of stakeholders. In this regard, Thomas M. Jones, Will Felps, and Gregory A. Bigley (*Academy of Management Review*, 2007, Vol. 32, No. 1, 137-155) worked out a segmentation criterion based on stakeholders' culture: agency, only viewing managerial interests; corporate egoist, only considering the organization's interests or short-term profit maximization; instrumentalist, acting "morally" only to the extent that it is profitable to the organization; moralist, adhering to principles regardless of whether they are profitable or not to the business, with a longer-term vision; and altruist, acting morally and following principles for the sake of others, on top of the organization itself.

Regardless of the segmentation model you choose, you must have one. You can build your own segmentation model based on whatever is strategic to your business. A segmentation model will help to allocate resources and define actions and objectives.

All this knowledge and management criteria should become operational in order to be really impactful on the organization and on stakeholders. A set of theoretical concepts without practical application would only serve the purpose of intellectual stimulus. The whole spirit of this book is to generate operational capabilities that can bring real economic value to the business. How can we turn all these concepts into day-to-day business practices? The framework I will present can serve managers operationally by creating and enacting a stakeholder management plan that follows these steps:

1. Define who your stakeholders are, based on their ability to impact your bottom line and their capability to spread your message and the reach of your activities and interactions.
2. Define the tone (positive or negative) of your relationship and the degree of your influence (little relevance to maximum relevance).
3. Classify and rate your stakeholders in terms of impact on business and visibility, based on relevance and tone of impact.
4. State clear and measurable objectives (enunciating them will define non-biased key performance indicators) in terms of how the relationship with each stakeholder will:

a. Determine the way the stakeholder, and other stakeholders, think about your company and its activities. (Positioning)
b. Transmit the knowledge needed for the stakeholder, and other stakeholders, to generate value to your organization. (Education)
c. Change via interactions through events and communications in a way that increases your organization's revenues and its opportunity to spread its messages while generating value for each stakeholder group.
d. Impact your costs, not only of managing each given stakeholder, but also costs influenced by your relationship with the stakeholder.
e. Improve your chances of increasing revenues. Revenue streams are the raw material of profits. Linking the relationship with a stakeholder to a revenue stream by means of an attribution model is key to determining the actual return (ROI) on stakeholder management activities.

5. Become operational through the assignment of responsibilities to a stakeholder manager, and through the definition of tasks, to be carried out by work groups.
6. Monitor results in real economic terms, on top of intangibles and relative performance.

How to Monitor Stakeholder Management Performance

The lack of a plan for managing stakeholders is at the forefront of the lack of a plan for monitoring results. Not having objectives represents the beginning of a trip to nowhere. Not having an evaluation plan is like heading to a destination without the ability to know when you arrive at it. Stakeholder management performance evaluation is based on two types of indicators: soft indicators, which originate in and impact each stakeholder group, and hard indicators, which originate in and impact the business.

- *Soft Indicators*

The perception of a stakeholder regarding a given organization is based on the stakeholder's evaluation of corporate social responsibility versus corporate social responsiveness. This perception can be measured using key performance indicators (KPIs) that monitor intangibles, or soft indicators.

Examples of intangibles and their relative performance indicators (KPIs):

Intangible	Performance Indicator
Trust	Trustworthiness rating
Transparency	Transparency rating
Ease of communication	Access to communication with the organization (yes/no)
Control of environmental impact	Awareness and compliance consideration (yes/no)
Commitment to a social cause	Awareness and commitment consideration (yes/no)
Fair trader	Awareness and consideration (yes/no)
Job creator	Awareness and consideration (yes/no)
Reputation	Reputation rating
Provides qualitative & enough information	Awareness and consideration (yes/no)

All these KPIs can only be gauged through relevant research. By relevant research, I mean, at a minimum, a survey completed by a representative sample of the population, which produces a minimum of 5% margin of error (to guarantee robustness of responses) and at least 90% confidence level (to guarantee relevance of the sample). This means that you must have a data collection plan on top of, or as part of, your execution plan.

Results of your data collection plan must show whether or not the goal of being perceived in a given way was achieved. They must also show the influence of the desired perception, such as transparency or trustworthiness, on either an income-generating act such as a purchase decision, or on the stakeholder's willingness to spread a message to other stakeholders. The degree of influence of such a soft variable on an income-generating act is the foundation of the decision-making pie on which to build your particular attribution model to convert soft variable inputs into monetary outputs.

For instance, imagine you are able to determine that the perception of your organization as seen as trustworthy has a 10% influence on a supplier's decision-making process to give your organization a discount. Then, you can confidently say that 10% of the monetary value of that discount can be attributed to your positioning efforts to be seen as a trusted company. Similarly, imagine if research shows that your commitment to controlling environmental impact has a 5% influence on a group of customers' decisions to purchase from you. You will then be able to attribute 5% of the profit generated by those customers to your education campaign about your organization's environmental efforts, assuming your campaign reached that group of customers.

Conducting research entails two types of complementary actions. First, quantitative research through a survey will provide statistically representative data with a known margin of error and confidence level. This approach guarantees the robustness of the attribution model and its credibility. Quantitative research is reliable for at least a couple of years, if most relevant conditions in the market remain the same.

During this period, you will be able to use the same attribution model and not bother stakeholders with tedious questionnaires. After that period, you can validate quantitative data through qualitative analysis using in-depth interviews. This second stage will help you to verify, in one-to-one encounters, whether the conclusions extracted during the quantitative research are still valid, at a much lower cost than the original quantitative research. It is recommended that you conduct quantitative analysis every three or four years.

Through thorough, planned, relevant, and rigorous research, organizations will build the robustness needed to embed credibility in their conclusions and attribution model related to soft indicators.

- **Hard Indicators**

Hard indicators are composed of two parts. The first is the isolation of the income-generating acts, such as purchases, that were impacted by stakeholder relationship management efforts, such as contacts, events, meetings, or media relations. The second is the influence of intangible concepts and interactions on each one of those income-generating acts. You must be able to translate relationship inputs – such as reputation, transparency, and trust – into the business outputs of costs and revenues. For this purpose, a robust attribution model supported by rigorous and relevant research, combined with consensus-based monetary conversion criteria, will feed the necessary data-generating business intelligence.

A Monetary Conversion Plan is the path to translate otherwise non-financial data into real financial figures. How much is trust worth? What is the opportunity cost of not communicating your transparency? If you did your research, you already have a decision-making pie for stakeholders' income-generating acts. The rest of the necessary information will come from your own company records.

One key piece of information is your organization's operating margin. "Operating margin," in this case, is sales revenues minus cost of goods sold (COGS). All other forms of margin will already include the money invested in stakeholder management (thus discounting the same cost twice when calculating ROI) and the efficiencies and inefficiencies of the rest of the organization, which are not related to stakeholder management.

Take the example of a telecommunications company that needs to manage its relationship with a city that is a key stakeholder. A survey indicates that every time the city awards the company a permit to install an antenna, its perception as a transparent company influences 8% of the decision-making process. If that antenna generates a revenue stream of $100,000 per year with a 30% operating margin, you could confidently say that the campaign communicating transparency has a return of $2,400 for this income-generating act. Then, add up all the returns generated by all antennas, as well as other income-generating acts impacted by the campaign. Subtract the actual cost of the transparency-communicating campaign, and you can calculate the actual return on investment (ROI) of the transparency campaign.

Part 4: Useful Tools

During our many years of experience and trial and error in several industries, the ROI Marketing Institute has gathered a set of very useful tools that will help managers save time and become more efficient in their quest to evaluate sales and marketing projects' economics.

The tools presented here are some of the tools used by ROI Marketing Institute and are meant to be used under the scope of the ROI Marketing Matrix. They do not represent any guarantee of success, nor will they deliver any specific results. Success, results, delivery, and value generation always depend on the operator and the quality of the information used.

Our intention in presenting these tools is to facilitate the use of the ROI Marketing Matrix and help managers and decision-makers work more efficiently by using them properly. The use of these tools can facilitate greater consistency and repeatability of evaluation cycles, objective assessment and comparison between evaluations, and easier access to information. However, there is also the risk of generating unrealistic expectations from the tools, as well as underestimating the time and costs of an evaluation and maintenance of a systematic approach to it.

These tools are intended to be used as they are presented, at the user's own risk. By using any of these tools, you acknowledge, accept, and agree that you assume full responsibility for each of the risks and dangers, and all other risks and dangers that could arise out of, or occur during or after, the use of any tool.

To download these tools, visit roimarketinginstitute.com.

ROI Marketing Matrix Execution Schema

Table 7: ROI Marketing Matrix Execution Schema

	ROI MARKETING MATRIX		
	Stage	**Action**	**Tool to Use**
ROI Marketing Cascade	Identify Pillars	Identify your organization's mission and vision, as well as overall marketing and sales plans. Aim to find the drivers of sustainability on three levels: economic/financial, social, and environmental.	Elicitation
	Set Objectives	Define performance indicators, period of impact, and success threshold in at least five dimensions of measurement. Align with the pillars.	Objectives template
	Relating Factors Plan	Define cause-effect relationships between marketing (messages and interactions) and business (costs and revenues) indicators. Isolate number of purchases impacted by the project and influence of project on each purchase.	Statistical analysis, internal consensus
	Monetary Conversion Plan	Define value or profit-per-unit-sold in cash.	Internal information systems
	Data Collection Plan	Use objectives indicators and define period of influence of project, data source, and data collection method based on project's dynamics.	Data collection template (3WH list)
	ROI Validation	Complete validation and predictive models for ROI Sensitivity Analysis.	ROI Sensitivity Analysis, historical data and evaluation checklist

ROI Marketing Ladder	Data Collection	Collect all necessary information to verify marketing plan impact on communications and on business.	Data Collection Plan
	Relating	Articulate your attribution model as defined in Relating Factors Plan. Establish cause-effect relationships between communications performance (project inputs) and business impact (project outputs).	Correlation methods (control groups, direct inference, trend line analysis, etc.), historical data, statistical tools, Relating Factors Plan
	Converting to Money	Establish the monetary value of communication impacts.	Conversion ratios from Monetary Conversion Plan
	ROI Calculation	Define the economic return of commercial and marketing investments.	ROI formula (net margin/investments)
	Conclusions & Analysis	Generate business intelligence from evaluation cycle. Set criteria for future planning.	Internal information systems (CRM, ERP, etc.)

ROI Marketing Matrix Objectives Template

Elements of an Objective – Each objective in the form must have the following elements:

- Indicator: What is that we are actually counting or measuring?

- Time frame: For how long will we be measuring?

- Quantity: What is the threshold that will tell us whether we achieved the objective or not?

What types of objectives shall we use?

- Positioning: what we want clients or consumers *to think* about our products, brand, or organization (e.g., our brand is cool)

- Education: what we want them *to know* about our products, brand, or organization (e.g., our products come in three colors)

- Interaction: what we want them *to do* based on what they think and know (e.g., sample the product)

- Costs: not only those directly related to the project, but also those that emerge from the project, such as discounts, commissions, etc.; also those that could be saved, such as by having fewer product returns, etc.

- <u>Revenue</u>: the isolated money inflows, mostly coming from sales, but could also be donations, for instance

- <u>Return</u>: the first time you conduct an evaluation cycle you will most likely not be able to set up objectives for returns, or they will be based on arbitrary criteria or assumptions.

Remember to validate your objectives with your reporting level or stakeholders prior to continuing with the evaluation cycle.

Table 8: Objectives Template

Project name:		
WHAT Performance indicator	**WHEN** Collection time frame	**WHO** Target of collection
Positioning indicators		
...	...	...
Education indicators		
...	...	...
Interactions indicators		
...	...	...
Cost indicators		
...	...	...
Revenue indicators		
...	...	...
Return indicators		
...	...	...

Name of the person who sets the objectives	Name of the person who validates the objectives	Name of the person who controls the objectives	Date of validation
...	...	...	...

ROI Marketing Matrix 3WH Data Collection Template

How to Use This Template

The 3WH framework (What, When, Who, and How) will facilitate planning for data collection. It is very important to plan for data collection and to then collect the data based on the plan. Many times, the complexities, the frenzy of sales and marketing projects, and the fact that execution depends on many actors prevent managers from implementing data collection as planned. Data collection is very important, and it is the only way marketers will be able to complete an evaluation cycle to calculate the economic return of projects and campaigns. The Data Collection Plan not only defines the information to be collected (the What), it also helps marketers define three other relevant sets of information:

When: The timing of collection is essential to guarantee the significance of the collected information. The wrong timing can lead to inaccurate or even unreal information, and therefore a lack of robustness and rigor that will taint results and conclusions.

Who: Choosing the right target to collect information from is key to obtaining relevant data. For instance, if you want to find out whether a doctor has learned how to apply a treatment, you should ask the doctors. But if the correct application of the treatment is supposed to not cause pain, you should ask the patients.

How: Choosing the right tool to collect information is fundamental to actual collection.

Remember to follow your plan during execution in order to gather robust data and foster credibility.

Table 9: 3WH Data Collection Template

Project name:			
WHAT Performance indicator	WHEN Collection time frame	WHO Target of collection	HOW Method of collection
Positioning indicators			
...	...	...	...
Education indicators			
...	...	...	...
Interactions indicators			
...	...	...	...
Cost indicators			
...	...	...	...
Revenue indicators			
...	...	...	...
Return indicators			
...	...	...	...
Name of the person who plans collection	Name of the person who validates plan	Name of the person who controls collection	Date of validation
...	...	...	...

You can add as many rows as needed for each type of indicator.

ROI Marketing Matrix Evaluation Checklist

Table 10: Evaluation Checklist

Project Name:				
Task	Concern/ Issue	Responsible person	When/ timing	Status
Set up positioning objectives	...	...	...	...
Set up education objectives	...	...	...	...
Set up objectives for interactions	...	...	...	...
Set up cost objectives	...	...	...	...
Set up revenue objectives	...	...	...	...
Set up return objectives	...	...	...	...
Establish Relating Factors Plan	...	...	...	...
Define Monetary Conversion Plan	...	...	...	...
Carry out Data Collection Plan	...	...	...	...
Calculate project break-even point	...	...	...	...
Validate project commercially	...	...	...	...
Run plausible scenarios	...	...	...	...
Check that data collection follows plan	...	...	...	...
Retrieve, tabulate, and analyze data	...	...	...	...
Build report	...	...	...	...
Report	...	...	...	...
Store business case and business intelligence	...	...	...	...

Appendix A:
How to Get Started

How to Get Started

Many roads may lead to integrating the ROI Marketing management model into any organization. ROI Marketing Institute (roimarketinginstitute.com) offers a variety of approaches that can help professionals and organizations of any kind to become ROI Marketing practitioners.

- *ROI Training Center*: In this initiative, professionals and organizations can acquire the first contact with and knowledge about properly measuring the economic return on sales and marketing investments. ROI Marketing Institute workshops are usually done on the premises of client organizations (in-company). There, participants and the organization get the most out of the knowledge that is transferred through real cases and that takes into account participants' real working environment. Workshops can also be conducted as open courses, where professionals can freely attend at designated locations and dates. Visit roimarketinginstitute.com for a calendar of these regular open workshops that anybody can join throughout the year.

- *Professional and Corporate Certifications*: ROI certification is intended for those organizations and/or professionals interested in achieving the top standard for ROI Marketing measurement knowledge and practices. It proves that the certified organizations or professionals have the proven capability to implement a set of practices and procedures that, if applied properly, will lead them to successfully measure the actual return on investment of sales and marketing projects and campaigns in a reliable and robust way.

- *Systems Integration and Implementation*: All good practices need systems that can guarantee implementation and delivery. Measuring the economic return of marketing and sales is no exception. ROI Marketing Institute consultants can help companies integrate practices or create systems that will ensure those practices are incorporated into standard operating procedures. It may or may not represent an additional technological layer. The working objective is to ensure that the ROI Marketing management model becomes a standard procedure within the organization.

- *Consulting:* This turn-key service is intended for organizations that would like to have an external source checking their marketing processes regularly, throughout a given period, with the aim of determining the economic return of specific sales and marketing projects or campaigns, or the level of adoption of ROI measurement practices.

- *Auditing*: This encapsulated service takes into consideration how a marketing budget was spent during a set period of time. It generates a competitive analysis that includes several performance indicators that help organizations understand how efficiently, from the economic point of view, the marketing budget was managed.

For more information, check roimarketinginstitute.com.

Tables & Charts Index

Table 1: Marketing & Sales Without ROI vs. Marketing & Sales With ROI 61
Chart 1: ROI Marketing Matrix Framework – Evaluation Levels & Measurement Dimensions 77
Table 2: Key Performance Indicators 80
Chart 2: ROI Marketing Phases 84
Table 3: Old vs. New Objectives... 99
Table 4: 3WH Data Collection Checklist..................................... 120
Chart 3: Trend Line Analysis.. 129
Chart 4: Relating Effects & Indisputability of Data 132
Chart 5: Revenue vs. Return 136
Table 5: Relating New-Car Feature Campaign: Performance Indicators in Each Measurement Dimension 149
Table 6: Indicators Monetization Reference Sheet..................... 151
Chart 6: Organization ROI Marketing Alignment 206
Chart 7: ROI Marketing Roadmap... 220
Table 7: ROI Marketing Matrix Execution Schema 246
Table 8: Objectives Template 249
Table 9: 3WH Data Collection Template 252
Table 10: Evaluation Checklist 253

www.ingramcontent.com/pod-product-compliance
Lightning Source LLC
Chambersburg PA
CBHW021353210526
45463CB00001B/97